POLITICAL CORRUPTION IN AUSTRALIA

'For the congregation of hypocrites shall be desolate,
and fire shall consume the tabernacles of bribery'

Job 15, 34

Political Corruption in Australia

A very wicked place?

PETER JOHN PERRY
University of Canterbury, New Zealand

Routledge
Taylor & Francis Group

LONDON AND NEW YORK

First published 2001 by Ashgate Publishing

Reissued 2018 by Routledge
2 Park Square, Milton Park, Abingdon, Oxon, OX14 4RN
711 Third Avenue, New York, NY 10017

Routledge is an imprint of the Taylor & Francis Group, an informa business

Publisher's Note
The publisher has gone to great lengths to ensure the quality of this reprint but points out that some imperfections in the original copies may be apparent.

Disclaimer
The publisher has made every effort to trace copyright holders and welcomes correspondence from those they have been unable to contact.

A Library of Congress record exists under LC control number: 2001090082

ISBN 13: 978-1-138-70278-3 (hbk)
ISBN 13: 978-1-138-63097-0 (pbk)
ISBN 13: 978-1-315-20706-3 (ebk)

Contents

Preface

This is not the book which I originally intended to write. That intention, to produce a comparative study of political corruption in Australia and New Zealand, has been superseded by the more modest, yet still considerable, target of an account of the phenomenon in Australia. Studies at this scale, and recall that Australia is a continent as well as a country, are relatively rare, an underdeveloped genre within a still rather underdeveloped branch of scholarship. The task in hand, the genre to be exemplified, is the short and introductory account of where political corruption is to be located in a particular country and how that situation was reached. The operation necessarily explores matters historical, geographical, political and social, to name but a few, but the result is not an exercise in any one of these disciplines. (Nor, it should be added, is it an attempt to establish a new one.) Rather it is an expression of dissatisfaction with the longstanding, albeit now diminishing, neglect of the phenomenon of political corruption by scholars, and an attempt to redress this situation at a particularly important scale.

Approximation is a better description than introduction. The book is concerned with the theme's gross anatomy, physiology and pathology rather than its fine structures, for that is all that is as yet possible at this scale and at this stage. My great hope is that it will stimulate more work, at a similar scale elsewhere and at a finer resolution within Australia. One obvious omission which already occurs to me is the absence of cartoons from this volume. The few on the subject of political corruption that are well known scarcely need to appear again, and an absence of time and resources prevented the necessary research to excavate new and cogent examples. There is a whole history of the subject along these lines ripe for the picking by someone with access to one or more of the great Australian libraries: go for it!

The weakness of the specialist base and the hope and expectation that the book will interest a wider audience, and not merely the handful of Australian experts in the field, account for the considerable element of more general discourse on corruption with which the book begins. It has not been thought necessary to reference this introductory material or the three final systematic and at times speculative chapters as fully as the empirical material of the central section.

Finally the title: designed to provoke rather than irritate or condemn, it is drawn from comments made by Parkes – eventually premier of New South Wales – on his arrival in 1839, and reported by Hancock in what became a very famous book in 1930. It thus links two very important Australians, a politician and a scholar whose thoughts in this area are still worth exploring. I added the sub-title and, more importantly, the question mark. And my answer is in the negative. Australia is not a very wicked place, but it does present us, and not least in its ongoing efforts to combat political corruption, with a range of experiences worth recounting for their substance, challenging in their demands on the apparatus and practice of scholarship, and highly relevant to the many countries now coming to grips with a real world problem which Australians are now tackling with exemplary energy and effectiveness.

Peter Perry
Christchurch, New Zealand

Acknowledgments

Individuals write books, but that enterprise is impossible without the support of family, friends, communities and institutions. When the book is put together in three places and over several years the duty and pleasure of saying 'thank you' becomes even more extensive. Firstly then the love and support of my wife, children and friends in Lyttelton and Christchurch is gratefully acknowledged, alongside that of colleagues at the University of Canterbury both in the Department of Geography (which also provided financial support) and more widely. They have been helpful, encouraging and tolerant. A period of study leave in 1999 took me to England, again with and to supporting and welcoming family and friends. In Cambridge I enjoyed the fellowship and hospitality of Clare College and the friendly professionalism of the University Library (especially of Terry Barringer in her position as librarian of the Royal Commonwealth Society collection). A visit to the Shelby Cullom Davis Center for Historical Studies at Princeton University proved both enjoyable and stimulating. At the most particular level Linda Harrison was as usual a most helpful and super-competent typist. The staff of Ashgate have been equally supportive. Three colleagues, Peter Hay (University of Tasmania), Len Richardson (University of Canterbury) and Jon Barnett (University of Canterbury) have read and commented upon drafts. Together we have made the book: responsibility for what it says remains with the author alone.

List of Abbreviations

ADB   Australian Dictionary of Biography

AEcHR   Australian Economic History Review

AJPA   Australian Journal of Public Administration

AJPH   Australian Journal of Politics and History

ANU   Australian National University

CJC   Criminal Justice Commission

HS   Historical Studies (after 1988 called *Australian Historical Studies*)

ICAC   Independent Commission Against Corruption

JRAHS   Journal and Proceedings of the Royal Australian Historical Society

NSW   New South Wales

PS   Political Science

SA   South Australiana

THRAPP   Tasmanian Historical Research Association Papers and Proceedings

WA   West(ern) Australia

1 Introduction

This essay is not a full continuous and complete account of every instance, facet and dimension of political corruption in Australia during the last two centuries. It is not even such an account from the traditionally catholic, wide ranging and usually empirical perspective of the discipline of geography. It would however be unduly defensive and misleading to describe or define it as preliminary or even introductory. Intelligent debate as to the events and situations it discusses has been going on for over two centuries, from the very beginnings of European settlement. For much of the period the discussion has been carried on inconspicuously and peripherally, but now, in an environment of aroused public concern as to the practical significance of the issues raised, it often possesses a high profile. Interim and approximate are probably the aptest qualifiers for this study; but what worthwhile research, in the eyes of either writer or critic, deserves any other appellation? The last and better word always remains to be said.

The beginnings of this project reside in three decades of teaching political geography in a New Zealand university, a period in which that sub-discipline has recovered from decay, disrepair and even disrepute to resume its traditionally strong position within geography as a whole. That revival is however open to the accusation – or so has been my experience – that it views the world through spectacles which if they are not rose-tinted usually filter out some of the more disagreeable facts of political life. It has rather little to say about dictators and even less about that corruption so characteristic of and central to their rule. Nor is corruption absent from the democracies though it is often well hidden, and likewise largely ignored. In other words there exist several and often related political worlds largely ignored not only by political geographers but by political scholarship in general. Those who ought to have been looking were seduced by topics much less challenging but more immediately and superficially rewarding such as elections. A short general book on political corruption from a geographer's perspective was my initial (1997) response: this piece is a continuation of the same enterprise at the macro-regional scale.

Why, then, the question must be asked at this stage, a book on political corruption in Australia? Is it really a very wicked place? Answer

1

– no. Does corruption in Australia really matter? Answer – yes. Why? Because it makes a difference. In the case of New South Wales in the latter decades of the twentieth century that difference embraces the gambling industry, public works, local government and coastal land development to list a modest selection of major issues. In these respects New South Wales is different from what it would have been under rule of law without disbenefit of corruption. Why disbenefit? Because while it is hard to disagree with the frequently made assertion that some particular acts of corruption in particular contexts get things done, that at least occasionally intermittently and fragmentarily it is a force for the better; yet on any cost-benefit analysis and in any rational consideration of a range of alternative courses of action – in other words at the meso or macro scale – corruption is generally less than optimal and not infrequently the worst course. In brief political corruption does not deliver, witness the third world, the communist world, and even Australia. Alongside these practicalities must be set the philosophical position magisterially articulated by Noonan (1984, 685-706): if we accept the arguments proposed by corruption's apologists can any moral ideal survive; do we really wish to normalise even elevate lying, cheating, stealing and deception as the way to do public business, rather than honesty, openness, justice, equity and compassion? My answer, and that I am sure of most Australians, is an emphatic no.

New Zealand is an unlikely base for such an exercise. It has a long standing and still mostly deserved reputation for clean government at both the political and administrative levels. This reputation is shared with a few other democracies, notably in Scandinavia. The other European democracies together with the United States and Canada are not quite so clean, in reality or by reputation, though well ahead of most of the third world and the former communist domain. Australia belongs with these democracies at least in broad terms, but comparison is complicated by the now high level of public awareness and hostility in the Australian case, manifest in considerable media attention. In much of Europe complacency, acceptance, and a high level of institutional hostility to enquiry prevail, eventually to be transformed into shock and horror. Moreover in the Australian case corruption is relatively insignificant in national (federal) politics and concentrated certainly and evidently at the intermediate (state) and probably at the lower (local government) levels. New South Wales in particular stands out not because it is especially or peculiarly corrupt nor because it has solved the problem, but because its Independent Commission against Corruption (ICAC) is both practically effective and thoughtfully innovative in a way rarely encountered elsewhere.

The boldness of this exercise soon became apparent. Political corruption is not a phenomenon to be laid bare by judicious reading of a few key secondary works or exploration of a narrow category of sources. It is too extensively pervasive, diffuse and yet deep seated. But Australian history and geography has always been marked by such boldness, even arrogance. A little over two centuries ago Australia was seized from its indigenous peoples for use as a prison and it was operated as such for more than half a century; it was then released into a version of colonial settler self-government which in half a century matured into a stable federal democracy. Nor is the boldness, even arrogance, and certainly courage of individual emigrants to be discounted as insignificant or eccentric. Most free settlers left the richest society in the world in the belief that they had even better prospects in a new and as yet underdeveloped world. That personal desire to do better, to get on and maybe to get rich, has to be incorporated into any understanding of the phenomenon of political corruption in Australia. In this context the position widely accepted during the latter part of the nineteenth century (Ward, 1963, 212-3) – and probably over a long period – that a distinctive Australia had no significant history is a matter for surprise. Few countries have so unusual a history.

The Problem of Sources

From the departure of the first convict fleet settler Australia was a well documented society. Corruption however is a major exception. Political corruption will always try to leave behind as meagre a paper trail as possible, and except to participants the verbal record will present similar difficulties. Fortunately in neither case is the exercise in secrecy, which is at the very heart of political corruption, and which raises one very central and rather curious methodological point (to be discussed later), anything like completely successful. Thus another surprise is to discover how well documented some instances have been. (But can one believe what was written down?) The result is not only the formal documentation of political corruption in occasional official enquiry and intermittent journalistic investigation focused upon political corruption, but also that which while primarily concerned with something else uncovers and explores this kind of malpractice. When it comes to the wider domain of historical scholarship, especially local history, and in such areas as memoirs, autobiographies and diaries, the problem shifts from paucity to potential superabundance compounded by the fact that such material discovers corruption incidentally to a more particular purpose, is rarely well indexed, and is often not indexed at all. However the absence of reference to corruption clearly ought never to be interpreted as meaning that the phenomenon was absent from that particular place or time. It may just have been very well hidden or the author may not wish to tar his topic with that particular brush, especially in a commissioned local history designed to celebrate rather than castigate. For example a history of Williamstown, published in 1969 (Evans, 1969) makes no mention of the 1930 Royal Commission which exposed (albeit without full publication) a high level of municipal corruption. The nearest to comment (182) is to record the high turnover of engineers in the city in 1931-2. Finally it is obviously impossible to read every Australian local history, government report, or newspaper. Any reader can examine only a small proportion of what might be relevant material and his or her explorations will inevitably contain a large component of the haphazard. Reduction of the problem by localisation in time or space is inevitably to sacrifice such important dimensions as overview and comparison.

The core of this argument is that except at a local scale the study of political corruption will always be flawed and incomplete by the standards of conventional scholarship. This is not a matter of moving in on the subject before sufficient detailed work has been done, but of the inevitable incompleteness of however much detailed work may be done. This work then rests on an incomplete exploration of incomplete evidence as well as of the secondary literature: as to the extent of its incompleteness it is for the reader to judge. The best it can attempt is to present as coherent an account as possible, a broad picture suggesting patterns and structures and illuminated by examples, indicating directions for future work, and hoping that someone will soon find a better way of undertaking such a study.

Australia as Microcosm

The introduction must not end on so thoroughly tentative let alone pessimistic note. The Australian experience of political corruption is of course unique, but it is also an accessible microcosm of wider experience. Not only is the two hundred years of well documented settler history a relatively manageable time span, but it encompasses an initial fifty years or so experience of strongly executive (even dictatorial) government; six brands of colonial self-rule quickly transformed into one federal democracy; a variety of relationships between several tiers of government; and an overarching context of rapid economic growth, population increase and social change. There are countries and regions where political corruption is and has been more important but few where its study is likely to be so broadly illuminating while remaining relatively manageable. The price, and as discussed the problem, is that of engagement with the history and geography of a whole continent. Political corruption is one, usually neglected, part of that history and geography. If it is unexplored our understanding of Australia is diminished; to explore it is not to assert a reductionist centrality. Rather it is to say that it belongs in any broad based examination of the continent, and to try to say where and why.

All this however takes us only to the end of the beginning. For quite different reasons the methodological issues arising in any study of political corruption, already alluded to, are not widely known. Nor are the basics of Australian history and geography. More must be said on both topics as an essential preliminary to the exploration of Australia's political corruption.

Issues of Method, Practice and Definition[1]

The word corruption has always had a place in both the popular and intellectual vocabulary of politics and a more general use. Until recently the popular place was very much the larger but the usage was almost always so general, imprecise (and not least polemic) as to be practically vacuous and remote indeed from the possibility of its scholarly application. Corruption is one of that class of words – fascist, racist, communist, and now sexy, are other examples – which effectively have no meaning because they mean exactly (or more often vaguely) what the speaker wants them to mean. In one sense the problem is easily overcome. A short and simple definition of political corruption can be given which is not vacuous, which limits the sphere of discussion without confining it too narrowly. What stands outside the boundary fence can still be talked about, but in other terms and other places. The agenda prescribed by such a definition as that of Alatas (1990, 1) – 'abuse of (political) trust in the interest of private gain' – and which I would regard as the best among a closely related cluster of definitions, circumscribes a substantial and significant list of intellectually challenging issues of great real world significance (Perry, 1997, chapter 2). In empirical terms two related issues require discussion: firstly the until recent failure of political corruption so defined and in more general terms to establish itself in the mainstream intellectual agenda – its perilously insecure hold on the edges and backwaters of scholarship (Perry, 1997, chapter 1); and secondly the problems which arise when the definition has to be applied in the real world, and when what is political corruption has to be distinguished from what is not. Meanwhile continuing use of the word with no thought as to its meaning provides intellectual confusion and irritation.

The most obvious and cogent indicator of the failure of political corruption to make the grade of academic respectability is the paucity of literature except in a few specialist areas, elections for example, arguably of secondary significance. Books on the subject are few, likewise papers in scholarly journals though their number has increased rapidly during the 1990s. The specialist journal *Corruption and Reform* now survives, after its short independent existence, only as an incorporation in 1993 into and sub-title of the journal *Crime, Law and Social Change.* Maybe it came into existence a little too soon? Encyclopaedias and dictionaries of the key disciplines more often than not have no entry or a very meagre one though useful exceptions exist. As lately as 1986 a book on *The Politics of Development in Australia* (Head, 1986) scarcely mentions the subject. The 1994 edition of *The Macmillan Dictionary of Australian Politics* (63-4) produces a resignedly cynical half-page on the topic for which some of the alleged cross-references turn out to be non-existent. A more substantial treatment of the conflict of interest component, though not of political corruption *per se*, appears in Lovell *et al.* on *The Australian Political System* in 1995. The contents page and index of most political science texts tell the same story, sometimes it must be admitted because the index is badly done but just as often because the assumptions and structure of the discourse scarcely allow for political corruption to be taken seriously. Beyond political science an army of texts in such disciplines as economics, sociology, and geography ignore or marginalise the topic.

Why is this the case? Why even now when political corruption is headline material for the quality media and has been so for almost a decade is the subject still so weakly placed and insecurely located in scholarly debate?

Firstly the purely practical aspects of the investigation of the phenomenon are obvious. Data collection will be at best difficult, at worst dangerous: potentially useful secondary material will as has been discussed be apparently inexhaustible. This is one reason why academics are at worst parasites (but at best commensuals) in their relationship with those who do possess the skills and special status appropriate for the direct investigation of political corruption, notably journalists. The journalist is able to look at corruption in a variety of ways not so readily open to the scholar, by being a ubiquitous presence as well as by going undercover. This is not totally to exclude primary or field study on the part of the academic. Petty corruption and the important area of public attitudes (Jackson and Smith, 1996) provide obvious instances. It is to argue the unlikelihood of the disappearance of that dependence on data collection by other professionals, or even by accident, and the primacy of the interpretative and reflective role (not that these are absent from good journalism) in the foreseeable future.

The second domain of difficulty is methodological and multi-faceted. Corruption brought to book is but part, a quantitatively uncertain and qualitatively imperfect part, of the totality. The relationship of part to whole is a fundamental problem. Bear in mind too that there are three sizeable bodies of corruption: that which is successfully uncovered and exposed – and thus essentially flawed; that of which we are aware but vaguely, imprecisely and uncertainly (save that we are pretty sure that 'they' are getting away with it); and that body of corruption, maybe large or maybe small, of even the existence of which we are unaware – and which is thus the perfect form. Really successful corruption is not simply undiscovered, it is totally unsuspected. We can never be quite sure that even New Zealand is as free of corruption as reputation and perception suggest. The alternative explanation of super-competent and thus invisible corruption cannot ever be ruled out. The methodological implications of this third situation are initially startling but at the practical level it is hard to see any operational significance except in terms of caution as to conclusions, quantification and measurement. Nor, I am quite sure, is this the reason why corruption is so understudied. The methodological issue is not one which most potential researchers appear to have considered very deeply.

The data for the study of political corruption is not only unrepresentative it is difficult. Reliable quantitative data is virtually unknown though 'guesstimates' are common. Court records, as to the number of persons charged with particular offences, are clearly a very modest exception to this statement and subject to the qualifications made in the preceding section. The stuff of evidence in this context is rumour, anecdote, memory, patterns of behaviour and lifestyle – fast cars and fast women! – and even bricks and mortar. For obvious reasons deceit, secrecy, misrepresentation, subterfuge and lying are of the essence of corruption. Again the scholar is not usually well trained to handle most of these kinds of issues: on the whole journalists, policemen and some lawyers and accountants are. It should be added that philosophers have also had relatively little to say on these subjects which might underpin or inform empirical scholarly investigation (Bok, 1978 and 1984).

A third direction from which to approach the question of lowly status starts with complacency. Especially in countries where political corruption is less than flagrant or rampant most people do not believe that it exists except at a small scale or do not want to know. The extent of political corruption is generally understated and underexplored; complacency is widespread. If the general ethos inhibits scrutiny so too and more generally the particular interests of powerful people compel them, not least by sustaining popular complacency, to keep the subject off the intellectual or any other agenda. 'Power tends to corrupt' and any effective investigation of political corruption will inevitably reveal 'wickedness in high places'.[2] The 'cover up' is the usual response, and if that fails then reference to 'bad apples' (rather than the barrels in which they reside), a reduction of the problem to one of individual morality which excludes other avenues of enquiry. On this point however it is too easy to be dismissive of the moral component. George Orwell (Shelden, 1991, 342) commends a 'moral criticism of society' – and note that like Noonan he is not moralistic – on the grounds of its revolutionary potential by comparison with politico-economic accounts which may well be nothing more than what is 'fashionable at any given moment' (and I would add place). It should also be added that this broad condition has begun to change. Tolerance and complacency have widely diminished, during the 1990s. We ought nevertheless to be aware that most of us continue to find it easier to condemn corruption in cultures other than our own than to explore the relationship between the idea of corruption and our own culture's way of doing things.

In parallel with a public complacency strongly supported by the particular interests of the powerful there exists an ideological dimension. In a loose sense this has already been alluded to, the structuring of enquiry within many disciplines can be such as to rule out a significant place or role for corruption. More particularly an uncritical Marxism denies the possibility of corruption in a Marxist state and, of wider significance, explanations of the present situation in many third world societies and economies solely in terms of the colonial experience exclude the consideration of corruption, whether driven from within or without, past or present, as contributory to the situation. At this point ideology connects with political correctness in the creation of a taboo present not only on the liberal left but also long enshrined in the working practices of for example the World Bank. The fact that Myrdal (1968) drew attention to the phenomenon from his eminence as a Nobel prize winner and in a widely read book appears to have had little effect. To use his own terms (938-9) for nearly thirty years 'diplomacy' usually triumphed over 'research' and the reversal of this situation remains incomplete. Finally there is the question of cultural relativism and the possibility of its use to explain political corruption out of existence as 'our way of doing things'. The apologist almost always speaks from a position either of power and benefit within the system or comfort outside it. Post-modernism may suggest, and at times merit, a similar critique. Yet it has also had no difficulty in proposing lists of civic virtues, justice for example, or emphasising the consistent and continuous application of rules as of the essence of justice, and in each case on a universal basis (Clark and Dear, 1984, 188). At least in their view the post-modernist has plenty of scope for consideration of corruption and the emphasis placed on plurality of discourses is one kind of safeguard against overgeneralisation or reductionism.

Temporal relativism raises another set of problems. Even if the definition is held constant the components change, and more significantly the context. The most obvious example and one relevant to the subject of this book is to compare British standards and norms of public life two centuries ago, the 'old corruption'[3] as it is usually called, which Britain exported along with the convicts to Australia, and those of now or of a century ago. The 'old corruption', tacitly endorsed as how politics had come to work, apparently accepted among other things confusion of public and private interest, patronage, procedural uncertainty, widespread payment of officials wholly or partly by fees with some uncertainty as to what the fee was and what it was for, and even bribery. However, this is not just a matter of 'old corruption'. Serle, writing of Victoria in the 1880s (1971, 271) notes the low moral tone of the colony and a general political ethic 'looser than now' (265-6). The observation 'that is how politics works' still not infrequently surfaces as something between apology, justification and description when the issue of political corruption is raised, especially in the company of journalists and media commentators, a century and a half after the alleged demise of the 'old corruption'. Similarly Williams (1999, 138-9) in the context of competing, contrasting and contested conceptions of liberal democracy raises the question of the extent to which leading and well known Australian investigators of political corruption – Costigan, Fitzgerald and ICAC – may be regarded as puritans or zealots. Several such arguments contributed to what is often described as the functionalist apologia or account of political corruption (Perry, chapter 9).

Finally mention of reductionism serves to introduce another group of issues. Political corruption is never the whole system rarely the dominant system, and usually a small part of a larger whole. It is a pathology (Friedrich, 1974) to use a commonplace term among many analogies (Perry, 27-8), albeit a contested one. To comprehend corruption we must understand what it is trying to subvert and likewise that there also exist alongside and between good government and political corruption as also between policy and practice such forces as negligence, incompetence, muddle and confusion. These four latter are rarely absent from any bureaucracy. They may operate in a fashion apparently similar to political corruption because the outcomes may be so similar in each case – for example a contract costing more than it ought – as to be extremely difficult to disentangle. Only too easily then can political corruption be invoked as the residual which completes the explanation and eliminates noise from the system. The world is not like that. Political corruption must enter the analysis only on the basis of evidence or strong suspicion and not in the cause of intellectual tidiness. This is a key point in the necessary effort to ensure that our investigations do not merely find not only what they are in search of, danger enough, but more of it than could possibly exist. Any methodology which lacks mechanisms imperfect as they must be in this context for restraining the investigator's enthusiasm for his or her subject or cause – a degree of inbuilt scepticism – is to be treated with disdain.

What is the relevance of this discussion to Australia? Certainly the practical problems exist, most conspicuously in recent years in the area of 'vice' as far as the risk of violence goes but also more generally. The Australian news media may be far from perfect but they have a reasonably good albeit uneven tradition of investigative reporting which provides ample food for scholarly thought. The methodological issues are in principle no different in Australia from anywhere else though Australians in particular are now exceptionally and unusually well provided for, in terms of both data and discourse, by a number of investigative bodies, most notably ICAC. On the other hand the powerful appear as prone both to corrupt and to cover up or in other ways to use their powers to inhibit investigation as in most societies. The taboo on investigation has probably always been weaker than in most countries, but the public level of interest and action has been far from consistent or insistent. Australians however are probably shrewder in their awareness of the situation and its implications, certainly than New Zealanders in their less infected condition, and also than Old World societies with a tradition of complacency and cover up. It cannot be reasonably suggested that political corruption ever took over from the official system save perhaps briefly in the two convict colonies. The arguable extent to which it is a threat to good government, a burden on the citizen's back and purse, and perhaps even a threat to the fundamental democratic order, is what this book is about.

The discussion to this point has provided neither a philosophically based nor a procedurally oriented method for the study of political corruption. Rather it is a list of cautions or concerns, explanations and evaluations, appropriate to an empirical account. I would go on to argue that as yet our understanding of political corruption and the extent of published work are both so limited as to make this inevitable. The development of more ambitious approaches must await stronger empirical and (as will be returned to shortly) definitional foundations even though these will in the last resort always be intrinsically uncertain. This is the case whether Australia or Zimbabwe is under discussion, but the fact that it is Australia that is being looked at here does introduce particular dimensions.

Alongside such considerations must be set the universals, the questions to be raised and the arguments to be explored whenever and wherever political corruption comes up for serious discussion. At least the questions, though not the arguments, are essentially simple. What causes corruption? What are its principal features? What are the main outcomes? Can we come up with estimates of its significance and its incidence? If corruption cannot be cured – and almost certainly it cannot – can it at least be controlled and reduced? Is corruption wholly a bad thing or are there times, places and circumstances in which it is functionally beneficial? Above all and as has already been noted what difference does it make? For if the answer is none then to study it is a waste of time.

Definitions

An examination of political corruption in Australia must explore these questions without expecting merely to traverse simple arguments and find uncomplicated answers and it must relate them to the real world of Australia's history and geography. In the process it will quickly and often encounter and re-encounter the question of definition, for it is one thing to articulate a cogent and coherent definition and another to decide what is and what is not an act of political corruption in a particular time and place. At a global scale this problem subsumes that of cultural and temporal relativity. The first is not the point at issue in the Australasian context given the cultural homogeneity of the settlers and, more surprisingly, the extent to which indigenous Australians have very recently taken on board a very Anglo-American concept of corruption and sought remedies in that context (ICAC, 1998 (2)). There remain considerable difficulties in exercising the definition already provided – and at this stage there is nothing better: 'abuse of (political) trust in the interest of private gain'.

The first and in this context most difficult component is that of abuse, explicitly of trust and it might be added implicitly of process. The corrupt individual hired and trusted to do one thing – to take decisions – in fact does another either on his or her own behalf or more often as an agent. This of course presumes that he or she knows what is the proper task, that the terms of employment (trust) are clear and likewise the rules and procedures. In all sorts of ways this simple statement becomes problematic in the Australasian context. Convict New South Wales was *inter alia* the export destination of the 'old corruption' in which administrative procedures were notoriously uncertain – and bear in mind the distance of the colony from its political masters – and the demarcation between private and public interest was although recognised certainly ill defined and erratically regulated. The engagement of officials in private enterprise alongside public business, often in closely related areas, was not in that time and place regarded as inherently corrupt. But when it presented a conflict of interest it readily became so. The problem does not disappear with the convicts and even though the bureaucratic process was gradually modernised. Public service patronage remained significant, in part for practical reasons, until at least the end of the nineteenth century, and nepotism almost inevitably raises the question of conflict of interest.

More broadly the position of the legislator in the area of development was especially difficult. He was and is expected – or more accurately was and is assumed – to think in terms of the general public interest, but also to represent the interest of his locality in that context and often against the interest of neighbouring localities – in say railway development – and in so doing it was and is unavoidable that he was and is also often looking after his own interest. In this context Lloyd's 1846 (183) observation that the sense of community in Australia was confined to 'local interests' and the observation that in 1912 the idea of breach of public trust was very novel (Prasser *et al.*, 1990, 14) are of considerable interest. As long as colonial parliamentarians were unpaid and especially before the party system developed, they were especially vulnerable though others would argue that the parties did little more than institutionalise the abuse, and the evidence that salaries solved the problem is contestable (Sachier and Storrier, 1965, 221). As recent cases have pointed out the formal terms on which he engaged in political activity – in the last resort the oath (ICAC, 1991 (1), 35) – also fail to resolve the problem. This is not to argue that every case of corruption raises such issues. Many are very clear cut. It is simply to point out that in this as in other categories there is a sizeable zone of uncertainty and argument.

The matter of trust has necessarily been substantially discussed in the preceding paragraph, but not quite completely. Two other elements can be raised. However perfect the rules at least part of the apparatus of government must be allowed discretion in its duties. The public servant is entrusted to use that discretion for the public good which may itself be attained by various ways although within defined limits. Secondly there is the question of intention. Breach of trust by accident, negligence or incompetence is not really breach of trust at all. However the element of intention, commonly regarded as integral to the idea of political corruption, is extremely difficult to prove whether as a judicial or intellectual exercise. As investigators of particular instances have discovered it is often difficult to disentangle such dimensions as corruption, negligence and incompetence. And these last two are moreover a fertile seed bed for the first. This is especially true when the public service possesses a large patronage element, when it does not attract the brightest and best, when the rules of government are rapidly changing, and when communication is difficult. All of these characterised convict and colonial Australia.

The political part of the definition appears more straightforward, having as its aim to set apart government business from economy and society at large, to distinguish political corruption from a larger body of crime and malpractice for reasons both of manageability and assumed distinctiveness and significance. The assumption is not entirely arbitrary even though the methods – bribery for example – may be identical. The political category clearly comprises ministers, legislators, judiciary and civil service. Some writers distinguish between the first two – as political corruption – and the latter two – as administrative corruption. That is not my usage, while admitting the existence of difference, on the grounds that the two categories are substantially interwoven and that the word administrative has a much wider and legitimate everyday use than as a synonym for public service.

The arguments advanced very recently by Williams (1999) that politics – the business of politicians – and public administration – the business of civil servants – proceed according to different and competing value systems deserve mention and exploration at this point. The activities of the former are necessarily competitive (as to a hitherto unprecedented extent they have also become in some restructured bureaucracies – another possible antecedent of corruption?) and the rules of the game are harder to codify and enforce. This needs to be recognised: judgements of the activities of politicians must be realistic. Politicians have expressed the same view in the context of the debate upon corruption. Greiner, premier of New South Wales, notes 'the conflict between the demands of politics and the demands of public office' (Philp, 1997, 437). However it is hard to dissent from the observation of Tiffen (1999, 2) also an Australian that 'there is no more basic issue than whether the governors are abusing their positions for partisan or personal gain at the expense of the public interest, or from Noonan's argument (685-706) that such defences of certain kinds of political action undermine any concept of political morality.

The limits of the category provide a further problem. What of the penumbra of occupations closely related to but not necessarily part of the civil service? Teachers and railway workers are two significant groups which in Australasia have until recently often been public servants in the strictest sense. What of those societies (usually communist) in which the state and the economy are almost one? In this latter case a broad but not unreasonable definition of political will make almost every misdemeanour an act of political corruption. Fortunately in the Australasian context it is only the first of these which is an issue.

Can we satisfactorily also circumscribe in terms of the nature of the action? Again the distinction is easily made at the extremes – the minister bribed by a defence contractor is corrupt, a state school teacher who absconds with the proceeds of a school concert is not. (Both are thieves.) This is a matter of the degree of centrality of the action to their task and trust. But what of the clerks in say a land registry who exploit deficiencies in the regulations or in local level management to line their own pockets at the expense of public or government in a way not hugely different from what they might have done in the private sector while nevertheless for the most part continuing the business of the department in an honest fashion? A possible alternative is to think in terms of scale: is there a threshold below which political corruption ceases to be significant? There is in fact a long recognised and important distinction to be made between grand corruption – say ministerial level – and petty corruption – say office boy level – but it does not solve our problem. Individual acts of petty corruption may appear insignificant but they are far from so to individuals on the breadline or in aggregate to society at large both in terms of overall cash flow or of the cumulative effect of distorted decisions in land grants or even street parking for example. The answer may lie in attempting to evaluate political significance even though that answer will be imprecise: ministerial actions are politically significant and corruption at this level can and should be addressed politically; running away with the concert money is not and cannot be. As to our hypothetical clerks political action is possible and is warranted if the character and extent of the problem is such that outcomes are affected significantly and recruitment, promotion, supervision and audit policies might make a difference. But it is naïve to believe that such changes will stop it ever happening or that occasional defalcation by light fingered individuals is sensibly regarded as political corruption – to reiterate it is mere theft.

The final component for consideration is that of private gain. Some parts but not the whole of this issue have already been considered. The most important omission is that of political advantage. Again it is a line drawing exercise: at what point does the cut and thrust of politics, dirty tricks included, become political corruption and can this point be fixed solely or primarily in terms of private gain? Office often, though not in every case, brings legitimate material rewards, to say nothing of the cases of manifest illegitimacy, but these rewards are rarely the driving force of high political ambition. To what extent too is the practice of rewarding supporters corrupt rather than inevitable and acceptable? In broad policy terms it is what we expect, and parties should expect to be pilloried for departing from their manifestos. At the other extreme awarding of contracts to supporters when their tenders are uncompetitive and their competence uncertain will usually be regarded as corrupt. As to the much researched pork barrel (Johnston, 1980), more favoured treatment of key electorates or of the home towns of influential members or supporters, judgement depends on how far the decision deviates from evident rationality. Recall there is usually more than one good site for a particular facility. This also illuminates the initial point of this section: political and personal issues must be looked at alongside rational and often technical considerations.

A related phenomenon of considerable contemporary import, Australia included, is that of party political finance. (As this section is being written the issue has dramatically surfaced in Germany.) Here the consensus is strongly hostile to corruption but the practical solution in an era of expensive media campaigns presents a problem. All means of financing political parties, individual membership, organisational (e.g. trade union or business) support, public funding are open to criticism. Parties may be necessary – though recent examinations of the alternatives have been few – but they are rarely popular. The issue is clouded by the fact that secret sources of funding have clear practical advantages to the parties as well as manifest dangers to the public interest and by the less well known but very well established fact that the corrupt financing of parties usually also involves a high level of payment to individuals (Perry, 68). Again discussion turns out to be useful rather than conclusive, and some startlingly and effectively innovative exercise in lateral thinking is anxiously awaited.

A second issue is the form of gain in more general terms. Political advantage has already been discussed and qualified. At the other extreme is the simple bribe – a cash payment and the most straightforward kind of corruption. There remain a number of other possibilities, a variety of payments in kind (from prostitutes to privileges – most of which can be translated into a cash equivalent) and the broad area of nepotism and favouritism. Two points need to be made concerning nepotism and favouritism. Firstly it is now usually against the rules in terms of appointment or allocation on merit and/or price. These rules however in many countries (and more widely in the past) conflict with custom. The Australian concept of mateship is a related issue. Note also that an increasing number of government jobs, essentially those of political adviser, now stand outside the public service system. To what extent if any should the concepts and constraints of nepotism and favouritism apply? Secondly most bureaucracies require decision takers to withdraw in cases where there is a close personal relationship with any of the parties, a rule and/or custom which is clearly in place to prevent both the suspicion and the actuality of corruption. At this point the significance of the word private as opposed to individual or personal comes into play. Many people will act corruptly in terms of a private world which includes an extended family or even a whole community. A further difficult question arising here is that of limits. The exchange of small gifts on appropriate occasions, business included, is a long standing and acceptable element in many cultures. At what point does it cease to be appropriate and become corrupt? Answer: when it goes significantly beyond established custom; when it is demanded or forced rather than freely offered; when its relationship to the business in hand is dubious; when it is secretive; when its monetary value is more than trivial in relation to that of the decision; and above all when it can be seen – which is rarely easy – to make a difference. On this basis the business lunch is acceptable, the sales conference or lobbying exercise may be, the Pacific Islands cruise is probably not.

Before proceeding to summarise this discussion and to present a *modus operandi* for substantive discussion two more theoretical issues need to be considered in their own right because they are of relevance to the Australian example and because they are often misunderstood and misrepresented. Over wide areas informed intelligent understanding of political corruption broadly coincides with and accepts the findings of specialist scholarship. We all have a pretty good idea of causes, consequences and controls even though our position and insight will differ in detail. The one exception is the argument that political corruption is unfairly represented as a threat to social, economic and political well being because it has in many instances provided a useful and effective mechanism for change in that direction, in other words the functionalist case. The argument is one still sometimes put forward with respect to the third world, more cogently and even at times reasonably argued for the New World, and especially North American cities, in the middle and later decades of the nineteenth century. It is also particularly applicable to the 'development' phase in Australia in the second half of the nineteenth century. The argument was at its zenith in the 1970s and the most powerful cause of its subsequent and substantial discredit has been empirical evidence initially from the third world but now more widely. Alongside this can be placed our increasing knowledge of the costs of corruption in monetary terms as well as indirectly, and our imaginative explorations of alternatives and counterfactuals. The basic functionalist argument is that corruption gets things done that would otherwise not have got done. But were they the right things? What did they cost by comparison with alternatives? What if the energy expended on corruption had been applied to making the established system work or changing it? Are the results really as beneficial as sometimes suggested? Over and above these questions there is the greater moral issue: if the functionalists' arguments are accepted in principle then no moral ideal can survive. What is the functionalist apologist's vision of the good society? There is clearly no room for consensus on these issues though the two sides might agree that corruption is functional at least in the sense that it is purposeful not accidental. In certain circumstances at the petty level that purpose – for example survival in much of the third world and in some of the communist societies of post-war eastern Europe – is entirely understandable and not morally reprehensible as far as most are concerned. One scenario to be feared is that the buzzword of the 1990s – accountability – will by mismanagement of its implementation unintentionally reinvigorate the functionalists' position. Corruption will become the only way to get things done in an overbureaucratic system. However the consensus largely deals with issues peripheral to the present day Australian experience which resembles much more closely that of contemporary North America where functional defences lack credibility.

The measurement of the extent of political corruption is notoriously difficult for reasons such as the pivotal role of secrecy and misrepresentation and the uncertain relationship of the discovered (and thus imperfect) to the undiscovered. Yet much of the preceding argument has proceeded along lines suggestive that it is necessary in operationalising the definition to think in terms of significance. That significance resides not in particular events but in overall outcomes – extending as far as public attitudes to the political system – and the relationship between the two is not always as might be expected. Firstly some people will act corruptly for rewards very small by comparison with the results, both immediate and more general. The sum involved in the incident which triggered events in Italy in 1992 was £3200 (Perry, 67). Less spectacularly the apparently small bribe on a large number of contracts, say the typical 4% on public works alleged to exist in New South Wales in 1991 (Maiden, 1991, 16-7), represents in total a large sum of money, a significant extra cost achieved at the expense of higher taxation or expenditure foregone elsewhere. Nor need corruption be ubiquitous to achieve significance: the mid-nineteenth century Australian pastoralist knew that freeholding a few key locations, notably where water was available, could secure control of a much larger area and the selector knew that the control of such sites could make pastoral occupation impossible. Again a particular and not necessarily expensive decision could have wide reaching and durable effects.

The definition of political corruption is then a matter for exploration and explanation. The old fashioned word bribe depicts the unambiguous heartland and the equally old fashioned graft the equally interesting penumbra. The limits of each zone are an individual scholar's judgement call as to what is worth pursuing and what is not.

Given that the idea of political corruption is simultaneously vague, polemical, obfuscated and contested, why bother with it? Might it not be better abandoned? Much of the difficulty is not intrinsic but arises from carelessness, controversy and unenlightened self interest. Not everyone stands to gain from an articulate discussion of the substance. For substance there certainly is, a core of illegitimate political practice of real world political significance but which our careless use of language has failed to distinguish from other domains of political irregularity. Making that distinction is often difficult but without it we will at best confuse and at worst ignore a category of political activity which while it is often disagreeable and deplorable constitutes a significant reality. This is an argument not for reductionism but for breadth. That is this book's aim, to add to understanding of Australia via the concept of political corruption and in the process to enhance our understanding of that concept.

Notes

1   For recent work in this area by Alatas (1993), Perry (1997), Rose-Ackerman (1999) see bibliography. Heidenheimer's (1989) handbook is the most extensive discussion, but deserves to be brought up to date.

2   Ephesians 6.12.

3   For a recent discussion see Harling (1996), chapter one. It is interesting to note the absence from the index of any Australian matter or of the words prison and convicts.

2 Geographical and Historical Dimensions[1]

Australia is preeminently the settler continent. This is not to deny the existence and durable significance of indigenous occupance. Nor, even in the context of political geography, is it to ignore environmental conditions even more different from those of Europe than their appearance indicates, the very substantial limitations of our understanding of which are a salient theme in Australian history and geography. Nevertheless Australia's political geography, one starting point for a consideration of political corruption, is a settler creation or more accurately a series of creations, and owes almost nothing to indigenous tradition and very little to environmental factors other than distance.

The initial political decision to colonise Australia was taken in London by men who never set foot in the continent. The direct British political input was dominant for more than half a century – the convict era – and continued until federation in 1900. But if the big decisions were taken in London a range of initially small though durably significant decisions on the continent's political arrangements had to be taken locally from the very start, and their implementation was an equally local affair. Philip's decision to decamp from Botany Bay to Sydney Cove was just the start. The range and scope of these decisions grew. If London set policy the new settlements organised practice.

A central concern of that practice was to execute policy in terms of human occupance, to make it work – not least by modifying it on the ground. This concern was initially dominated by penal issues but it also embraced such matters as survival in an unfamiliar environment, the more or less orderly occupance and distribution of land (the distant forebear of contemporary land-use planning), the choice of sites for central places (as already noted), a degree of economic management, and some contribution to and regulation of the provision of infrastructure. All of these were grist for the mills of administration, legislation and litigation, for honest, even heroic, government. But they also provided opportunities to deviate from the straight and narrow, occasions which we call political corruption, to say nothing of muddle and confusion, individual incompetence and negligence, and unforeseen circumstance.

19

Distance

A salient and subsequently controversial component of that process was the question of distance. Physical communication with London was at first a matter of months or even years, with a dash of uncertainty as to success. Only in the last thirty years has it been reduced to the instantaneous. As to information the telegraph provided an immediate flow of admittedly expensive information (at first to the cities and then more widely) from various dates in the nineteenth century. The first service was established in 1854, complete inter-capital connection in 1876; and the link to Britain and Europe in 1871. The home government was at no time in a position to undertake day to day management and nor, a matter of equal importance in the corruption context, could it easily or effectively discipline the personnel of the colonial administration. Even the ultimate sanctions of dismissal or recall would take at first years and later months to implement. Meanwhile the show had to go on. All kinds of political misbehaviour might proceed almost unchecked from the mother country: any effective checks and controls must of necessity be local. At this point and in anticipation it should again be noted that the whole ethos of British government as at first exported to the colonies and particularly as New South Wales was settled was ambivalent as to political corruption: the 'old corruption' was alive and active, though under more and more criticism, and patronage British and local was for even longer the method of making almost all appointments.

The factor of distance as already mentioned worked in a comparable fashion within Australia even though the striking fact of a high degree of population concentration in urban centres (and especially colonial – later state – capitals) is evident from the start of European settlement. In most of rural Australasia the public service infrastructure was geographically remote and expensive of access. It could only too easily be ignored or by-passed and, more significant in the corruption context, the activities of what public service did exist was difficult to regulate, monitor or discipline. A dishonest public servant or a determined settler could expect to get away with a great deal and for some time. Moreover, and to continue the parallel with the London relationship, not every element of colonial government policy was well tuned to the real world of farmer or miner or even to the growing pains of the state parliament's own urban back yard. The fundamental spatial relationships of both convict and colonial Australia facilitated political corruption.

Personnel

Colonial and penal Australasia was also overstretched in terms of personnel. Each colony planned, proposed, or was compelled to do a great deal with a very little. Populations were small by comparison with the extent of territory and the tasks which had to be undertaken to survive and to grow. There was a real shortage of expertise, not least in a bureaucratic profession which at least initially was the rationale for very few emigrants, alongside a deal of energy, enthusiasm and determination. Political energy had for the most part to be provided after the exhausting business of making a living in pioneer society had been accomplished whether in terms of the working day or a working lifetime. In these circumstances it was also often difficult to distinguish between public and private interests. Few could spare the time to pursue a parliamentary career even though parliamentary sessions were short and those who could, typically successful men of business, would stand to benefit more than most from the obtaining of government funds for local development. Moreover it was *inter alia* to advance the interests of their community in the contest for scarce resources that they were elected. More recent concepts of conflict of interests and the appropriate response collide with common sense and the broader public interest in such instances. This is not to say that there were no real conflicts of interest in such contexts, rather it is to state that the operationalisation of any definition be it of conflict or more broadly of political corruption, is neither simple nor straightforward. This was especially the case in the colonial and development period, approximately the second half of the nineteenth century, but it has parallels in the convict era. The argument but not the practice or excuse has lost most of its cogency by the second half of the twentieth century.

Environment

Settler Australia had to come to terms with and to occupy a peculiarly difficult environment. The Aboriginals had succeeded in this respect but at a cost and by a process of transformation as well as adaptation, and on terms hard to translate and incorporate into the settler experience. To confuse the issue superficial similarities to Britain – the fact that what grew in Britain could be grown in Australia – concealed profound difference notably in terms of sustainability. Both the timing and forms of European occupance as well as hard won experience necessitated political management not so much of the environment *per se* as of the process of occupance, even if until recently such policy has sought more often to protect the settler from himself or his fellow settler than the environment from the settler. At times the policy has been incisive and effective, the promulgation of Goyder's line (1865) as the limit of crop farming in South Australia for example. At others insight has run far ahead of public opinion, in the area of possible and viable population growth in the 1920s for example, pitting a geographer Griffith Taylor against a horde of ill-informed politicians. In every case of conflict the possibility of getting round unwelcome rules and regulations by corrupting minister or official – 'the habit of leaning on the bureaucracy' (Davies quoted by Encel, 59) – has existed. Through much of Australasia's history such situations would not have been viewed primarily or even at all in environmental terms even though the first major political decision taken in the continent – to shift from Botany Bay to Sydney Cove – was an act of environmental policy. In fact a great deal of mining, land and infrastructural legislation and regulation is aptly, albeit not exclusively, viewed in such terms. At the start of the twenty-first century the politics of the environment is conspicuously mainstream, institutionalised in the planning process, and more than occasionally the domain of corruption. In brief the assertion that the Australian bureaucracy finds one of its several tap roots in the need to manage human occupance of a new and different environment certainly deserves our consideration.

Settlement

The development of Australia since 1788 is the story of agricultural, pastoral and mining occupance of a quite small proportion of the continent's land area. It is thus also the story of extremely rapid city growth which has always accommodated the greater part of the population. In this latter respect the Australasian experience is at its closest to that of the rest of the New World and not completely divorced from that of the mother country. Political corruption is a familiar and significant component of the process of rapid urbanisation though at least in Australia and even in its most rapidly growing great city – Melbourne – not the whole story. Nevertheless the development, the very geography of those cities, cannot be described or explained without consideration of political corruption, particularly in infrastructural provision, water, railways, refuse collection for example, and more recently in land-use planning. It is also in the cities that the seemingly intractable problem of police corruption in its intimate association with a group of industries often summed up in the word 'vice' (including prostitution, drugs, alcohol and – perhaps misleadingly – gambling) has its roots, of very long standing, and its most frightening manifestations. Without this macédoine of corruption the geography of Australian cities would be quite different. The idea of the counterfactual 'what if?' is basic to the geographer's interest in the topic.

Finally if Australia is a discrete land mass it is also a defined political entity, component part for a century now of the global state system and previously of a global empire. What is now one state (possibly even a nation state) was previously six political entities of a different (colonial) kind of which only one – Tasmania – was defined essentially by its geography; just over two centuries ago it was a political entity of another quite different kind. The five states of the Australian mainland are moreover arbitrary creations, made necessary (as occupance proceeded) by forces of distance and difference, their limits for the most part geometrical.

Settlement possesses a number of strands of variable durability and differing interpretation but it would be hard not to admit at least the possibility that the relative cleanness of South Australia owes something to the role of organised company settlement, that Hancock's assertion of a vague unmeasured (convict) inheritance (41) is particularly relevant to New South Wales and Tasmania and cries out for reinterpretation rather than rejection, or that the circumstances of the nineteenth century mineral bonanza in Victoria may have something to do with its different experience of corruption by comparison with Queensland and West Australia. A simple geographical account of Australasian political corruption is simultaneously an exercise in initial brief description and a set of important questions. However that geography must be considered alongside and in connexion with the continent's history.

Government

The British took control of the Australian continent from 1788 as a military operation which as far as possible ignored the rights, if it could less readily ignore the presence, of an indigenous people. New South Wales was a peculiar and low status colony albeit a very large one. It was a prison with very little thought given to the possibility or eventual inevitability of free settlement, to the status of convicts at the end of their sentence, or to economic and commercial issues in general. They were certainly not going to get a free ride home! The lowly political and administrative status of the colony owed something to two decades of war following immediately upon initial occupation. During this period the Caribbean, Canada, the

Cape, and even tiny possessions such as Malta mattered: on the whole New South Wales did not, even half a century later; 'a paltry colony' as it was described in 1830 (*Hansard*, 11 June 1830). Nevertheless it was a colony and as such possessed an administrative apparatus: a military establishment and a convict establishment – soon to be merged – and a slowly emerging apparatus for dealing with the affairs of free men. For half a century it was an executive state, at times a *de facto* military dictatorship, dealing with two distinctive albeit connected human conditions (free and convict); it was also possessed of an at best erratic and at worst feeble judiciary (the branch of government most hampered by distance from Britain) while almost devoid of representative legislative institutions. This is not to exhaust the distinctive features: some historians, most notably Atkinson (1997) for example, have emphasised both the 'ubiquity of government' (87), and its Enlightenment roots which embraced at once the renewal and the commodification of human lives (38). The tensions and contradictions in this position are evident: convict New South Wales was at once brotherhood, dictatorship and oligarchy.

As to the other Australian colonies three distinctive experiences of European settlement can be recognised. Tasmania (Van Diemen's Land) was an early penal satellite of New South Wales, and became a separate colony in 1825. In proportion to its size Tasmania received many more convicts than New South Wales, and transportation continued longer. The two other large eastern colonies, Victoria and Queensland, also began as parts of New South Wales, in the first instance as settlers reacted against the official policy of spatial containment. Their eventual separation owes more to the antipathy of a rapidly increasing free immigrant population to the idea of a penal colony, and to the problems of administering half a continent from Sydney. They were also, sooner in Victoria and later in Queensland, colonies where great mineral wealth was to be found. Finally South Australia and West Australia represent settlement outside the New South Wales umbrella, determinedly different and decidedly – in the case of South Australia emphatically – free of convicts. West Australia was only reluctantly a penal colony, between 1850 and 1868, to counter a labour shortage. Both were highly, though in the case of Western Australia somewhat incompetently and unluckily, organised company settlements. South Australia is the antipodean epitome of this style of settlement although they were more numerous in New Zealand.

Colonies to Commonwealth

Only in New South Wales and Tasmania among the earlier colonies was there a long period of non-representative and highly executive government of a distinctly autocratic kind and with a powerful military presence. Western Australia's later experience of such a system was a matter of its tiny population and its failure to attract free settlers in any number until the mining booms of the last decade of the century. The other three colonies were settled, especially in their period of rapid expansion in mid-century, in a clamour of demand for representative government which they shared with their two older neighbours and quickly obtained. The demands were conceded with a generally good grace and each colony was equipped with a bicameral legislature, a judiciary, an executive, and a London appointed governor who was by no means a figurehead. Only West Australia, remote, penal and very small had to wait, finally achieving representative government in 1890. In essence the colonies had internal self government while Britain looked after foreign affairs. The level of political involvement of the governor and of reference of business to London gradually diminished: the course was set towards the present status of the Governor General and six state governors, constitutional monarchy by proxy. The detail of constitutional arrangement was similar but not identical in each colony but each was a Westminster in miniature, an application of that experience in a thinly populated context where even on a liberal suffrage electors would be numbered in hundreds rather than thousands or tens of thousands. There was always a shortage of able people in government, members, public servants, judges. Two colonies were both larger (save in spatial terms) and faster growing than the others – New South Wales and Victoria. The former had the early start but the resource base of the latter – essentially gold and thus rapid population increase – made them comparable in many measurable respects if different in many others during the second half of the century. They and their capitals were of course to become intense rivals.

Almost as soon as local self-government was achieved by the six colonies consideration of unification in the form of federation began. The inconveniences of separation became evident – three railway gauges for example – as well as the incongruity of six sets of political institutions in a large and thinly populated continent. Differences of size and of economic interest and outlook – Victoria was more often protectionist than New South Wales – did not prevent the achievement of federation (the Commonwealth of Australia) by 1900. Predictably the federation left the states intact, in possession of most of the powers and tasks which they had as colonies, and also of their distinctive traditions. The Commonwealth had by comparison to devise new ways for a new political entity. One remarkable dimension of this tradition is the apparent absence of political corruption by comparison with the state level. That Australia is a liberal democracy Westminster style can be taken as read, but a rather noisier version at the federal level, at least in public. The states present an even more rumbustious version, historically as colonies struggling heroically to establish Westminster style standards and norms, ways and means, on or near the frontier, and even now looking at times ragged at the edges and disreputable at the core. Their political corruption has exposed as it has rested upon a degree of democratic deficit in state legislatures and state elections. The centralist and executive tradition has been strong in the Australian states *ab initio* a surprising phenomenon in that period of difficult communications. It must again be recalled however that right from the start Australia was a very urban society, its population concentrated in state capitals. In those cities state government had a local feel to it and was often concerned with what is handled municipally elsewhere, education and health for example. The two facts of the existence of state government and the concentration of population go some way to explain the traditional insignificance and as Hancock notes (273) late arrival of local government in Australia, the great cities to some extent and ironically excepted. But it is not the whole way.

Economy

Penal

The context of Australian political corruption is not solely that of political but also of economic entity and experience. As a starting point consider the fact that convict Australia was an exceptionally unproductive society. Little of what it consumed was produced in the colony – the resource base was at first poorly understood and the labour force infamously unproductive – and so a very large albeit slowly diminishing proportion of what was consumed was imported over very long distances. From the start the tertiary sector was large and its geography was predominantly urban. What it existed to manage was, in concrete terms, trade and a highly peculiar, in the concrete sense a penal, labour force. More abstractly government managed scarcity and inequality. It operated via a public institution of military origins – the commissariat – with some degree of monopoly power and minimal formal public input. The institution dealt in basic commodities, grain and meat for example, and used its authority to convert others, most famously and most profitably rum, into a similar status and even a currency. The legal framework of the penal colony in general was uncertain and incorporated a great deal of gubernatorial patronage as well as individual discretion – except of course for the convicts. But all prisons are run at least as much by inmates as by officials and New South Wales was no exception. Rather it was an extreme instance. Convicts from very early and of necessity occupied not only menial but also important administrative positions, for example in the commissariat. Altogether New South Wales was for at least several decades a very peculiar economy and society indeed and Van Diemen's Land even more so, albeit for a slightly shorter period and in a relatively peripheral situation. Where to fix the social and economic limits of convict and ex-convict economic social integration rapidly became a central and divisive political issue and often subject to change with the arrival of a new governor.

Pastoralist and Farmer

The intention to severely restrict and closely regulate the spatial extent of the penal colony was subverted by the discovery that the country was excellent for grazing sheep, the merino in particular, and for the production of fine wool. As a non-perishable and relatively high value commodity wool was Australia's ideal and initial staple export. The grazier required access to cheap land, capital, some degree of official recognition of presence and position, but only modest security of tenure. He sought a licence to occupy a large and loose domain rather than the freehold of a small and well defined area and his investment in improvements such as a house and yards was typically modest and localised. The terms on which these 'licences' might be granted by government scarcely featured in the planning of the colony: they were necessarily a central concern of most governors, a problem with no simple, single or durable solution. The grazier – more often known as the squatter or runholder – slowly found himself or herself (the lady was not quite unknown) in competition with settlers who wished to farm more intensively, to grow grain or keep cattle, though in terms of property size still on a very large scale by British let alone European standards. Legislation and administration had to be put in place, and kept in working order, to manage the competitive allocation of land for both purposes, a matter for both personal choice, rational decision and political process. The matter was also one of durable if even now imperfectly understood environmental significance. Unsurprisingly then rural land and its politics will feature conspicuously in any discussion of corruption in Australasia.

Mining

The second great resource base of Australasian economic development was the continent's mineral wealth. Traditionally pride of place has gone to the Victorian gold rushes of the 1850s and they certainly highlight the beginning of large scale exploitation of the continent's vast and varied geological resource base but only a beginning. Western Australia was similarly projected into rapid growth by gold discoveries near the end of the nineteenth century. Coal, bauxite, iron ore and oil are among the pillars of the Australian economy a century later. The industry is now almost wholly a matter of big and usually international business: there is no room (and only briefly was there ever much room) for the individual or even small group. Historically and geographically however their enterprise was significant out of all proportion to duration. Mining has however been less central to the study of corruption in Australasia than might *a priori* be expected. The temptation is to assume or expect corruption in an activity which is at once speculative and lucrative and it is not hard to find instances. Certainly the best documented, and of great political significance, is the Mungana affair of the 1920s (Kennedy, 1978). Corruption occurred and continues to occur when mineral multinationals meet state ministers. Sharp practice was ubiquitous in the flotation of mining companies in the nineteenth century and is by no means unknown a century later – but sharp practice is not the same as political corruption. On the other side of the picture consider the fact that mining was a very public as well as a very regulated business, especially in the gold rush context, and that well founded accusations of political corruption were a major cause of the Eureka Stockade (1854) which resulted in the creation of an equitable, efficient and public system of mining regulation and some reform of policing. This is to at least begin to explain why mining features less centrally than land in any discussion of corruption in Australia.

Development

The word development and its frequent use are almost unavoidable in any discussion of Australia's geography and history. Beginning with convicts and subsistence the story does not come to an end with sheep and gold. Some indication of its continuance and extension has already been given as both the traditional core areas have diversified. Other sectors have a long history but enter the picture later than sheep and gold, the manufacturing industry for example, and a third group, of which the tourist industry is an excellent example, are phenomena of only the last few decades. None of these developments could have taken place without the infrastructures appropriate to their needs. The oldest such category was roads and bridges, historically the most important was railways. Some have been rather taken for granted and others too easily ignored, urban water supply and sewerage for example. All of these and others represent a large capital investment, an inevitable competition for resources, and the necessity for political control at colonial/state and/or local government level, both of initiation and operation. They are all of them areas, though not a comprehensive list of such areas, where political corruption has been evidently present. The public service also dealt with areas already mentioned, land and minerals, as well as their offspring, land-use planning and environmental concerns in general and with newly discovered areas of political concern, indigenous land rights for example. Each and every one of these has at some time and place experienced the phenomenon of political corruption as well as present exercises in its exposure, discussion and reduction. It should be noted at this stage that in this respect Australasia resembles the other parts of the world, especially North America, which underwent similar if far from identical development experiences during the last two or three hundred years. However this is not the whole story of political corruption or Australasian political corruption. Parallels and comparisons are to be actively sought in the third world, where a development component in the manifest presence of political corruption is apparent, in the communist and ex-communist world where authoritarian institutions and scarcity and shortage suggest interesting parallels, and not least with the developed European countries which having shed the 'old corruption' maintained for more than a century the pretence that nothing like it had taken its place. The recent collapse of that complacency if not of the hypocrisy indicates that something very substantial and not unlike the Australasian experience has developed and is going to prove rather more difficult to deal with than its distant Antipodean cousin.

Some commentators have discussed Australasian political corruption or even political history at large in terms of a development paradigm. Fitzgerald's history of Queensland (1982 and 1984) is a stimulating example. Given the principal locus of the phenomenon at state level differences in the development experience and ethos of the several states, both past and present, require comment. Western Australia and Queensland can be held up and discussed as examples, especially in their recent history, of development at almost any price and of consequential political corruption. This is crude oversimplification but also suggestive of explanation. At the other extreme penal New South Wales was shackled, though not successfully, by an official anti-development policy: when development came it was a matter of opening up the colony and its trade. Victoria had no such shackles and its development in the second half of the nineteenth century was begun by gold and manifest in rapid metropolitan growth. From this arose the intimate connexion between its development and a policy of protectionism. For South Australia development meant farming and mining but also the protection of its distinctive cultural identity, and for Tasmania the constraints of a size and resource endowment modest by mainland standards. Development thus provides an attractive paradigm for an account of political corruption in Australasia. However it is not only incomplete but must take into account the diversity of geographies, histories and economies which exist not only within the Commonwealth as a whole and as salient features of those political and geographical entities within Australasia – states, municipalities, counties, districts and so on – where political corruption is more evidently present. And so once more we draw close to the broader areas of methodological and definitional debate and analysis, a territory replete with intellectual and practical problems already discussed.

Conclusion

Finally two related points must be made. Political corruption occurs within a geographical and historical setting but is always in the last resort a matter of individual and group decisions which were never, even in extreme cases, quite inevitable. It is however appropriate to make this point later rather than earlier because so often the individual is employed as a sole or predominant explanation of political corruption and thus as an explaining away beyond the realms of rational enquiry or remedy. Bad apples have featured too often and bad barrels have been ignored. Both must be taken seriously. All the latter categories depend however in the last resort on the existence of the former – men and women prepared to break and bend the rules in their own interest. If members of this category rarely appear to be in short supply yet a much larger proportion of the population – all of the people some of the time and some of the people all the time – kept or tried to keep the rules often when to do so was not in their own immediate interests or when the rules were not good rules. The numbers or proportions are impossible to estimate. Australia was made by these two opposing forces: neither a reductionist account in terms of corruption nor its counterpart of honesty is adequate.

Given then the context of two hundred years of settler occupance on a continental scale what are the topics and issues which particularly deserve attention? What agenda, given that an agenda is a selection of priorities as well as a plan of attack, is appropriate? The modifications of the 'old corruption' by Australian conditions to produce an initial local version is the obvious starting point, leading to examination of the commissariat and the assignment of land and labour as activities which had a durable impact. It is however important to recall the role of free settlement and to look beyond the penal colonies, to those areas on their margins which were to gain separate colonial status, and to the quite separate and more distant company colonies. Colonial and development Australia, on a narrow view the experience of the second half of the nineteenth century and on a wider view lasting until at least the 1940s and on the wide view to the 1970s was in some ways the antithesis of its immediate antecedents – free, en route to independence, rapidly expanding. That expansion embraced land settlement, the creation of infrastructure, and in many areas the mineral resource base, each of which possessed a corrupt dimension and within which can be considered other issues such as the persistence of patronage. Two world wars provide abrupt interruptions to this situation yet in many ways the habit proved persistent, the continuities more marked than those of the mid-nineteenth century. And much of the corruption exposed and explored in the last two decades, in the broad and important area of public works, differs little from its late nineteenth century equivalents. Other areas represent evolution: land remains an important area of corruption but in terms of planning rather than settlement and with connexions to the broader issue of resource management. Here questions of the vast increase in the scale of corruption and its significant internationalisation as new developments take place become evident. This is not an exhaustive list of issues. There are hardy perennials to be fitted into our territory: vice; local government in general and city government in particular; and lastly the methodologically oriented issues such as the links between political parties and political corruption and the question whether in the development context, especially of the second half of the nineteenth century, corruption was so inevitable and so clouded a concept and actuality as not to deserve the name. The primacy which this approach seems to give to time periods over spatial differences must not be exaggerated: what is being presented is a story – it is also a mosaic, and mosaics can be very telling representations of reality.

Note

1   For general historical and geographical background refer to Bolton (1986-88) and Jeans (1986-87). The parliamentary sources are extensively but inconsistently listed: the best starting points are Hagger and Montanelli (1980) for the Commonwealth and most states and Zalums and Stafford (1980) for West Australia.

3 Convict Australia[1]

Political corruption came to Australia with the four convict ships which dropped anchor in Botany Bay in 1788. Whether the concept is applicable to indigenous Australian society before this date is an interesting methodological point beyond the scope of this book and the competence of this author. The same is true of the similar appellation of the whole process of seizure of the land from its indigenous occupants but it has already been noted that indigenous Australians are now actively aware of its applicability to aspects of their present situation.

To connect Australia's political corruption with its convict origins is to make no great intellectual leap or discovery. In practice it has often been to narrow the focus of discussion, and at worst to make the question simplistic and to extract it from the broader context in which it belongs. A thorough enquiry must begin by relating convictism both to its penal character and to its roots in late eighteenth century British society, recognising that most convicts were simultaneously criminals and victims. This in turn introduces the essentially paradoxical character of the penal colony. Then and only then is a meaningful discussion and interpretation of the particularities and details, the picture in the frame, possible and useful.

The peculiarity of penal Australia, of the first half century of New South Wales and Van Diemen's Land, can scarcely be exaggerated. Nothing like it has ever taken place elsewhere: a whole continent taken over by armed force, though the armed force required little use, to serve as a prison, albeit a prison whose principal bars were the oceans, for the world's most advanced industrial society ten thousand miles away. For almost fifty years ordinary civil government was only a part, and for a long time a small part, of a system in which the penal component, the colony's *raison d'être*, and the military establishment, were pre-eminent. These were of course themselves part of government but their methods and priorities were distinctive. As an export of the English establishment of their age no part of the system could reasonably be expected not to be corrupt; prisons and the army and the public service were part of the 'old corruption'. Moreover on the broader scale armies and prisons have a perpetual and ubiquitous reputation for corruption and corruptibility regardless of their larger political context. A degree of corruption in prisons is almost independent of the degree of political honesty of the society of which they are part. This is usually regarded as an expression of the fact that corruption is fundamentally connected with and an expression of inequality and that prisons are intrinsically expressions and institutionalisations of extreme inequality and extreme control. But to make prisons work, and even such unusual prisons as those of New South Wales and Van Diemen's Land, a degree of give and take between powerful and powerless is required and corruption, the breaking and bending of rules in return for a variety of favours, is part of that process. The forward momentum of this situation is rather different from that which will be discussed in the context of patronage and decision taking. The argument in this case takes the form that it was in penal colonies, and in terms set by their penal character, that the distinctive and durable relationship between state and society in Australia was established. Because of its penal context the relationship was both incipiently and actually corrupt. Australia was able, like Britain, to cast off as it outgrew its several skins of 'old corruption', but the abolition of transportation could never eliminate the formative experience of the convict period.

The military element was rather different. Its effect was generated, its momentum provided, not by a fighting force but by a small army of occupation and control with time on its hands and an early acquired reputation for greed and venality. Again the near universal reputation of such forces in this respect should be noted. Greed and venality certainly underpinned the high level of military (and occasional naval) entrepreneurial activity displayed most actively, but certainly not exclusively, by the officers of the New South Wales Corps, activity which went beyond that typical of an army of occupation and was generally in breach of regulations. Of more lasting significance was the central role in the life of the penal colonies occupied, again for about half a century, by the military commissariat, an institution discussed in detail below.

The argument to this point is then that any study of political corruption in Australia must begin with the penal period, but in broad rather than narrow terms. The morality of both the convicts and the convict system needs to be moved to the margins without however quite forgetting that the phenomenon of political corruption rests upon a set of individual moral decisions. Nor must it be forgotten that in some respects, most notably the assignment of convict labour to free employers, transportation was one of the most effective forms of penal rehabilitation ever to operate (Hughes, 1987, 586). Assignment was both inevitable and effective in terms of cost, a low rate of reoffending and high rate of rehabilitation. The problems it resolved, in a Draconian fashion now both impracticable and unacceptable, remain to plague much of Europe and North America. On the long term view transportation was a corner stone of one of the world's most stable democracies.

'Old Corruption'

It is wholly unsurprising that the 'old corruption' characteristic of late eighteenth century Britain was exported to Australia, and equally unsurprising that it underwent a sea (and land) change. Convict Australia was essentially an administrative and executive order, at times almost a dictatorship. Administrative is a word used advisedly. Politics and political activity were not unknown but in the absence of representative institutions they were very secondary, in marked contrast to what quickly became the case after such institutions were granted in the middle of the nineteenth century. Thus some of the best known dimensions of Britain's 'old corruption' were largely absent from Australia, notably electoral corruption and a range of activities connected with parliamentary business. Other elements are absent for different reasons, the sale of offices and the associated business of sinecures (Jackson, 1998, 10). Generally speaking official posts in convict Australia were not bought and sold and their occupant carried out the duties in person even while also often engaged in business in contravention of official regulations. In the case of senior posts patronage was exercised at a senior level in the Colonial Office. 'They will job colonial appointments in Downing Street' was one despairing comment in 1826 (Eddy, 1969, 29). Bathurst, Colonial Secretary in London from 1812-27, coupled an unusually long period in office with a particular love of patronage, arguably delaying its diminution, and he was active during the post-war period when large numbers of unemployed officers, variously qualified, sought jobs (McLachlan, 1969, 481), a burden to be added to the long standing practice of pulling strings to use the colony as a dumping ground for 'troublesome connections' (Phillips, 1909, 11). For a much larger number of middle and lower ranking positions patronage was located within the colony and often in the hands of the Governor. In almost all cases the evidence suggests that it was a matter of connections, contacts and favours – in a small pond – rather than cash. It must also be recalled that the 'old corruption' operated relatively openly and though already fiercely criticised was to a degree still either acceptable or ignored. It might at this point be argued that even though the patronage system of convict Australia links up with the 'old corruption' it was not political corruption in the strict sense: it was just how things were done in Britain and thus in

New South Wales. This functionalist argument has some force but is weakened by such matters as the incompetence and dishonesty of some of its products (Eddy, 1969, 29 and 194-5). Take for example Evans, Surveyor-General in Tasmania who took up office with a reputation such that Macquarie, the Governor, was officially warned to keep an eye open against 'peculation of the public property' (Robson, 1983, 66). In practice Evans was technically incompetent – 'not a plan or sketch was to be depended on' – eminently bribable, and busily engaged in getting land for his family (Robson, 1983, 194-5). Complaints from the top as to problems in finding good men continued throughout this period. Gipps commented to La Trobe (McCulloch, 1959, 31): 'though I am almost tormented out of my life with applicants for office, I never know when I want a good man where to put my hand upon him'.

The pivotal role of patronage within the 'old corruption' Australian style expressed itself not only in jobs but also in the allocation of key resources. This is especially the case with respect to land and convict labour – the latter the process of assignment – where in the absence of any kind of plan and under pressure of need these resources were allocated, the former in its abundance and the latter in its scarcity, on the basis of favouritism, nepotism and connection. In some cases this was in flagrant breach of such rules and regulations as existed and from an early stage both elements of the policy – if such a name it deserves – were the subject of frequent criticism. The third major element of resource allocation – the commissariat or government store – also belongs in the patronage tradition not as a matter of adaptation to unforeseen need but rather, at least initially, as a matter of deliberate planning. As a government and military operation the military commissariat was the obvious procedure for provisioning the settlement even if it soon developed distinctive and peculiar characteristics. Given that government and military were vessels of the 'old corruption' it is impossible to envisage that the commissariat would be established and developed on any other than patronage lines. Such a course of events seems, in retrospect, equally unlikely as far as land and assignment were concerned but it could never have been quite ruled out as a possibility. And in practice arbitrary and commonly corrupt land allocation gradually gave way to more orderly and open, if certainly not corruption free, procedures which were an important role of government in the colonial period. With the end of transportation assignment died a natural death.

All three questions – land alienation, labour assignment, and commissariat – were highly bureaucratic. The clerk features almost as conspicuously in early Australian history as the convict, and the fact that he often was a convict was frequently condemned ('Bigge Report', 1822, 103-

4 and 157). The bureaucracy however was a manifestation of the 'old corruption' tradition in its several dimensions rather than of its modernised version to which the term more properly belongs. Patronage was one of these dimensions, but of even greater importance in this context was the absence of clear and public and consistent rules and procedures for the conduct of public business (Parsons, 1974, 7-8). A related feature was a certain seeming vagueness as to the distinction between private and public business. Many officials were also in trade, sometimes in breach of regulation, and failed to separate this activity from their official role. Nor was it the case that officials at any level could rely upon their orders being carried out by their subordinates.

The 'old corruption' thus contributed to an ethos and an environment in which both bureaucracy and irregularity flourished and coexisted, providing very favourable conditions for the establishment of distinctively Australian versions of political corruption. There was of course geographical variation: the opportunities afforded by Sydney were different from those of rural districts. Likewise different régimes, since the system enforced no uniform way of running government in the earlier decades, had different outcomes. The meticulously detailed rule of Governor King (Atkinson, 1997, 237-8) (who claimed he knew where every nail in the colony belonged and was to be found) was succeeded by Governor Bligh whose erratic rule appears to have been exclusively verbal (Atkinson, 1999, 274). Nor were officials at any level necessarily consistent in their own behaviour; King took decisions to his own personal advantage (Baalman, 1962) while at the same time he was on a broader front engaged in a programme of reform and rectitude (Barnard, 1962, 84-8).

This situation was of course ephemeral, brought to an end by the end of convict transportation, massive free settlement, responsible and representative government and the demise of the 'old corruption' in the mother country. Its span was little more than half a century, but it was modern Australia's foundation half century. Political corruption was part, and a durable albeit adaptable and flexible part, of that foundation even though the latter part of the penal period witnessed a substantial diminution of those forms most closely linked with 'old corruption'. The overall significance of the penal experience in Australian history, as well as its politically corrupt dimension, remains a central concern of Australian scholarship. However, before that issue is addressed some flesh must be put on the bare bones laid out above.

Land

Of the categories and questions discussed above land, and especially land
alienation and settlement, is the most problematic. In the absence of any
clear or explicit, let alone overarching land policy, at the start of settlement,
the period until 1831 is one of at best policy made and changed on the run,
and at worst of chaos, conflict and confusion (Roberts, 1924). The idea of
corruption presupposes system and order and when these are weak then so
is the idea of corruption and its usefulness. Yet the word may reasonably be
used to characterise, at least in part, the non-system which prevailed prior
to Ripon's 1831 reforms. It was a discretionary system of grants (and in
some cases quit rents) without purchase but sometimes with guidelines. Its
elements of corruption embraced at least the following: favouritism,
deception, breach of instructions, although of course to call every instance
of irregularity an act of corruption is to assume a usually unprovable
intention. In brief responsible officials did not distribute land equally or
equitably or even in relation to the applicant's ability to make good use of
it. Officials favoured themselves, their families and their friends, and
perhaps those who lobbied most vigorously. They lied in their applications
and in their response to conditions imposed on them. The problem was
persistent: Therry (1863) writing a personal memoir of the later convict
period entitled one chapter 'The prevalence of perjury'. Such mendacity
may in many cases have been reprehensible – it is not quite corruption.
What can reasonably be assumed is that much lying was so patent that the
generous bureaucratic response even if not always based on such
considerations as friendship or influence (let alone the simple bribe)
constitutes an act of corruption. The same is true at least in part of failures
in such areas as imposition of conditions or collection of quit rents
(Morgan, 1992, 7-8). Note that this activity was the task of magistrates and
survey officials, neither of which groups enjoyed a high reputation.
Townley for example (1991, 51) describes much early survey in Van
Diemens Land as faulty both in execution and registration. Land
transactions which should have been documented, and in some cases,
reported to London were not (Ward, 1987, 290), a situation again very
strongly suggestive of corruption. None of this occasions retrospective
surprise: if it was not always and invariably a manifestation of 'old
corruption' it was the kind of behaviour, often with a substantial element of
inconsistency, that the 'old corruption' might be expected to engender.
Recall in particular the failure clearly to distinguish and differentiate
between public and private interest. It is also apt to reflect that if such acts
of corruption laid the particular foundations of long term problems yet their

absence – a hypothetical but not impossible context of strict adherence to the law when there was one and inaction when there was not – would have produced merely a different chaos.

Probably best known among all the instances of corruption in land alienation is the well known deal between Bligh, King and Mrs King in 1806-1807. King as governor granted Bligh 538 hectares and next year Governor Bligh granted Mrs King 316 hectares. The transactions were manifestly corrupt inasmuch as top officials were putting through deals in their own interest on a scale of which London would not have approved and which the parties had not in fact reported (Baalman, 1962). A generation later in Tasmania Governor Arthur resisted Ripon's land reforms which ended grants and introduced sale by auction (Burroughs, 1967, 62-3). Such resistance to orders was not uncommon. Goulburn as Colonial Secretary in Sydney is probably the best known case in his failure to carry out Governor Brisbane's orders and his favouritism towards the exclusionist party (*ADB*, 'Brisbane', 153). In Arthur's case this attitude was combined with a hard line on petty corruption (Forsyth, 1970, 53) and a personal involvement in land speculation assisted by Montagu his Colonial Secretary (Townley, 1991, 46) in Hobart Town on the basis of his own access to information and his own decision taking role. His Attorney-General, Gellibrand, was an active land jobber (Robson, 291). On other occasions officials defended their own interests on a similar basis by the policy of obstruction. A third example is provided by Acting Governor Grose (1792-4) who broke the rules relating to land grants by giving his friends larger than permitted grants near towns and who also defied the rules and good sense – again in favour of his friends – relating to the width of streets in Sydney (Barnard, 70-3). In this case corruption left a conspicuously permanent mark. Lastly the conspicuous corruption of the Survey department, central to land settlement, requires specific mention. For example surveyor Dangar in 1827 simply took 1300 acres for himself and his brother (Barnard, 1962, 274), and some subsequent improvement was not sustained (McMartin, 1983, 236). Over and above staff shortages, low pay and a confused legal framework the venality of officials, especially in Van Diemen's Land and at the most senior level, is evident. This was a matter not only of their professional activities – or more accurately unprofessional – but of their private speculations. The same is true of the Treasury at least in Van Diemens Land. When after seven years incumbency the misappropriations of Treasurer Thomas were exposed the official enquiry reckoned the deficiency at £10627 (Shaw, 1967, 138-9). Note however that the experienced Bigge regarded the equivalent department in New South Wales as incompetent and confused rather than dishonest (Barnard, 1962, 326). Nevertheless Survey ranks alongside Commissariat as the institutional seat of corrupt practice.

Until at least the 1820s the climate of opinion and activity scarcely favoured reform. The first serious attempts to do so, undertaken by Governor Darling 1824-31 (Fletcher, 1979), indicate an expert and perceptive assessment. They included: insistence on the priority and primacy of public duties; replacement of convict clerks as unlikely to resist temptation; advisory land boards (surrendering also his right to assign labour) (Therry, 1863, 133); provision of salaries in the postal and customs services; and particular measures such as cessation of revenue handling by the Survey Department and an enquiry into the Treasurer's investment of government funds, leading to reprimand. Centralisation was deemed desirable where possible. Darling did not solve every problem, nor was he entirely consistent or even necessarily entirely honest, though then as now accusations of corruption were part and parcel of the political vocabulary and armoury of the opposition.

Labour

The land was useless without labour to work it and the necessary labour was under government control. The assignment of labour was in theory a rational process related to the quantity and quality of land and the skills of the individual labourer, skills useful on the land only in the case of a minority, and useful in a specialised sense – those of craftsman or mechanic – for an even smaller group.

On the surface at least assignment was a more open and honest procedure than land grant, and of course closely connected to it. It could have worked well. In practice such was the political and administrative climate and the variation in quality that prospective employers sought to manipulate the process, and in this the 'favoured few' (Therry, 1863, 134) succeeded. 'Mechanics' were reserved for 'very particular favourites' in New South Wales in the 1820s (Atkinson, 1826, 51), and in 1832 half the skilled convicts in Van Diemens Land were employed by one tenth of employers, mainly officials (Hughes, 1987, 287). Bigge had attempted reform directed 'to secure the performance of it from the operation or the suspicion of corrupt and partial views' (Bigge, 157). Ephemeral as the system was, ending in 1838, it served as another instance at a formative period of the corrupt power of a privileged few *vis à vis* the government. Not every verdict however has been hostile. Alongside its corrupt dimension must be placed some degree, how much is debatable, of practical success: 'the most successful form of penal rehabilitation that had ever been tried' (Hughes, 1987, 586). Economic assessments are less favourable. Maconochie, not it must be admitted an impartial critic, reckoned its inefficiency, a compound of graft and waste, as one and ninepence in every three shillings (Hughes, 1987, 490-1). To summarise: a means of using convict labour which would have been fairer and more efficient is not inconceivable, but what was put into practice should not be written off as total failure.

Commissariat

The commissariat, like land and labour, was peculiarly colonial though not peculiar to the convict colonies. At home it was a small part of the military bureaucracy, of minimal importance outside that domain: in New South Wales and Van Diemen's Land it was the central economic mechanism for almost half a century. By 1810 it was issuing rations to half the population and buying three-fifths of the settlement's wheat (Phillips, 1909, 8). The commissariat began life as the stores branch of the convict colonies of New South Wales and Van Diemens Land. Such bodies existed, but lacking the penal component, in all military bases and thus all colonies. Who in London was actually in charge? War Office, Treasury, Colonial Office, Home Office all had a stake and there was plenty of scope for inter-departmental hostilities (Butlin, 1994, 60) especially between 1812 and 1827 when Bathurst presided over the Colonial Office. The period through to 1815 was further complicated by frequent reforms made necessary not by the Australian experience but by the exposure of inadequacies concomitant with the Napoleonic War. Simultaneously, and again unforeseen and unintended, the commissariat expanded to meet the colonies' peculiar needs from simple store to become market for buyers and sellers, importer, bank, and credit agency controlled by a small group of officers and officials. That these men converted a vital public institution into a vehicle of private profit is again unsurprising: the inability or reluctance to clearly demarcate in such areas was another salient feature of the 'old corruption'. Colonial commissariats and army stores never enjoyed a high reputation for honesty. It is rather the scale of the transformation, the penal colony as the lucrative and near monopolistic business of a small élite, that justifies its discussion in terms of political corruption. Like labour assignment and unlike land alienation the commissariat was of relatively short term direct significance. When transportation came to an end in New South Wales in 1840 and Tasmania in 1852, so did the commissariat's importance enter a speedy and terminal decline. However it was the core of the economy for half a century and over and above its tangible, if as yet underexplored, consequences it shared with patronage and the processes of land alienation and labour assignment in the formation of Australian attitudes.

The government (originally military) store or commissariat as a central colonial institution was not an Australian peculiarity. One secondary reason why Bigge was chosen to report on the convict settlement in 1822-3 was relevant experience in Trinidad's commissariat (Ritchie, 1970, 49). Nevertheless the Australian experience if not the institution was as has been noted peculiar and in many if not all respects disastrous. In the two penal colonies, and because they were penal and nothing more, the commissariat was exceptionally dominant and, as already noted, diversified. Even when its status was eventually clarified (in 1813) it was weakly regulated, especially between 1812 and 1827 (Butlin, 1994, 59-60). Bills drawn on the Treasury in London were always honoured (Boot, 1998, 77) and became, together with commissary receipts, one element of the colonial currency.

In New South Wales the commissariat got off to a better than might be expected start in the hands of an able and honest officer Palmer (*ADB*). He was however demoted by MacArthur in 1811 by when corrupt practice had spread. This was in part the result of a period of rather tenuous London control in 1808-9 (Boot, 1998, 77), but also because of the role of convicts as labourers (Bigge, 1970, 42) and clerks – the better educated with 'an air of authority and presumption' (41) – and customers. The institution had also come under the control of a clique of officers, officials and their friends. One of their motives may have been beneficial, to break the East India Company's official monopoly of the colony's trade, and this was certainly the case with respect to the flow of funds into the colony allowing a wide range of government activity (Boot, 1998, 80). Their central intention however was a new monopoly in their own interest and on the basis of what Butlin (1994, 66 *seq.*), whose explorations of the institution were both thorough and shrewd, regarded as 'improper conduct'. This included organised theft (as servant), beneficial pricing (public interest sacrificed to private), kickbacks, fraudulent records, bills issued to self, illegal use of government property, irregular travel and forage claims (these last still prevalent in the last decade of the twentieth century)[2] and the broadest of profiteering. Thus, in this latter case, the price of sugar at least doubled and may have gone up eight times as it passed through the commissariat, and of calico four to five times (Atkinson, 1917, 535-7). More generally Boot (1998, 84) characterises a rather later period,

Darling's governorship 1825-31, in terms of conversion of public assets to private use by public servants. Others have given a quite opposite perspective (Rose, 1922, 170).

There was a beneficial side to this diversion of the commissariat from the traditional mainstream of more petty military corruption. What actually occurred brought the undoubted benefit of financing Australian growth at Britain's expense (Butlin, 1994, 67), and was pivotal in the transformation of New South Wales from isolated gaol to a free market economy (Statham, 1990, 45), a benefit compounded by Treasury laxness. But the commissariat officials and clique in establishing the bolder course of a whole stream of subterranean public finance were in breach of instructions. Their 'privatising of the colony' (Butlin, 1994, 69) – again the terms sound almost contemporary – came at a price, the selfish manipulation of scarcity, privileged access for the few and extortion from the rest. This situation generally favoured officials and military as men of business over independent farmers, and merchants over producers, and with the advantage of access to official funds for unofficial purposes – again the confusion of public and private interest. It was all too good to be true and is almost surprising to learn that from such a privileged base four senior members of the commissariat failed financially between 1814 and 1822, Drennan for the large sum of £6500. He had a track record of this kind before his appointment to Australia. Broughton, their successor lacked a strong enough patron to reach the very top but his reforms favoured the small settler (Reinits, 1967, 33-44) and Darling's reforms transformed the commissariat for its remaining decades (Fletcher, 1979, 259). It was still enormously powerful, employing half of all government clerks in the late 1830s (258) even as the changing state of the colony rapidly reduced its importance.

To regard the commissariat and its corruption as a combination of the ephemeral and the functional is too dismissive a position. For almost half a century it was the branch of government with which the citizen was most likely to come into contact either on terms of privilege or, more often, disadvantage. In either instance it provided in the long term an unfortunate basis for a developing relationship. The government could be manipulated at a price, and the government was both untrustworthy and unavoidable. The commissariat system in its corruption favoured large scale entrepreneurs, whether as landowners or merchants, over the small settler or tradesman, setting the scene for an ongoing theme and problem.

Convict Stain

The idea that the convict stain is one simple explanation (among many) of ongoing political corruption in Australia has never quite disappeared. To argue a simple connexion and direct descent is to extend the limits of credibility. Representative governments in the colonies took over an apparatus for land alienation and settlement which having inherited a muddle was on the way to its resolution. The particularities of the convict period – unrecorded and unmeasured grants, an almost incredible multiplicity of procedures, a confusion of private and public business – had for the most part disappeared. Corruption had not, but it is not well considered as a direct descendant of the penal experience but rather as an evolving response to new circumstances and opportunities loosely connected to a different and detested past. The fact remains that the greatest of Australian scholars, deploring oversimplification of the kind outlined above, remain insistent on the formative character of the convict period and while not explicit on the issue of corruption it is hard to imagine them rejecting any role for it. Thus much quoted is Hancock: 'all the clues which seem at first sight to suggest the visible persistent influence of convictism … prove in the end to be misleading … Yet we may suspect that there has come down to us, by subtle hidden channels, a vague unmeasured inheritance from those early days' (Hancock, 1930, 41). More briefly but no less eloquently Butlin (1994, 196) remarks 'many of the original ingredients hang over the rest of modern Australian history'. What? Why? How? The convictism-corruption connexion as inheritance and ingredient requires some discussion.

Just as the broad issue of the nature of the convict colonies remains controversial so too there is no consensus as to its durable significance in the domain of corruption, a domain which is as yet scarcely explored. The nearest approaches reside in the broad view, attacked by Hirst (27), that the convict masters – the ruling class – were corrupted by power; in Barnard's note that irregularity (225) was the rule; and perhaps most cogently in Butlin's view (1964, 108) that a great deal of convict crime was 'adapting and perfecting a market system that did not fully meet their needs', almost a functionalist account of corruption. What is more generally available is a range of aphoristic or epigrammatic comments on the penal period which suggest both antecedent and momentum. Thus McMartin (1983, 4) emphasises detailed control and Atkinson the government's function as universal provider (Atkinson, 1987, 116). His picture of the intellectual bases of convictism, as already noted is far from wholly benevolent (100-1). A new sense of political responsibility was in his view intimately accompanied by new methods of subjection. The phrase brotherhood and dictatorship (134) is even more suggestive of the tension. The whole of Atkinson's interpretation is antithetical to any emphasis on the 'old corruption'. Ward's evaluation (1987, 283) of penal New South Wales as 'absolute state socialism' instantly connects to a mainstream of enquiry and opinion relating to political corruption. Barnard (1962, 68) interprets the outcome in a propensity to look to the government for everything while remaining a hostile critic; Maconochie in 1838 commented upon impatience and irritability as a typical attitude (Forsyth, 1970, 165) even towards well meaning government. Charlton (1983, 31) quotes Shapcott: 'the mentality of convictism, with its master-victim overtones is still pervasive: it goes right through the system, and it runs through the attitude of people towards each other'. And this is in a book on the Queensland 'state of mind'. Even Hughes (1987, 596), while warning of the dangers of convictism as a shadowy behavioural catch all notes 'the familiar habit of cursing authority behind the back while knuckling to its face as a lasting legacy. Collectively these interpretations and observations suggest that the public response to a very peculiar and intrinsically corrupt system of government possessed attributes which remain typically Australian – the government as a benevolent, unreliable and wealthy 'aunt', not especially well liked but simultaneously unavoidable and exploitable (by fair means or foul) in a relationship fraught with tensions and inconsistencies.

The Other Settlements

The convict colonies were but part of both the continent and its history during the period prior to the end of transportation and the granting of responsible government. Victoria and Queensland, originally parts of New South Wales but beyond the pale of substantial penal settlement and vehemently opposed to its extension, and the two free colonies, South Australia and West Australia, whose history scarcely impinges on that of the rest of the continent until federation, all require discussion. The crucial dates in the case of Victoria and Queensland are 1824 and 1836 when European settlement began and 1855 and 1859 when representative government was granted. European settlers came to West Australia in 1826 and South Australia in 1836 receiving representative government in 1856 and 1870. Except in West Australia responsible government soon followed. West Australia received a very large number of convicts in the 1850s.

Queensland and West Australia require least comment. Only 23 years after the beginnings of European settlement Queensland received representative government. It was still a small colony, at least in terms of population, practically devoid of convicts (the core of the separatist issue) and as yet of much knowledge of its mineral wealth, a backwater of pastoral expansion. Note however that its most distinguished historian Fitzgerald argues for an ongoing and extending momentum of convictism: a class interpretation of the colony's history (1, 92) with plenty of space for corruption. Likewise there were seemingly inevitable scandals over land sales in the early period (1, 93, 189). Queensland however quickly gathered momentum. West Australia where settlement began in 1826 remained moribund until the 1890s, victim of isolation and a difficult environment. The response to the modest flow of population which resulted was, reluctantly, to bring in convicts in large numbers, but few analyses of the experience suggest that this was the main root of corruption even though Forrest, an early and distinguished premier, ascribed to it a broad significance (Crowley, 1971, 14). Likewise the commissariat (Statham, 1984). Rather corruption owes something to the interaction of the conservative values of many early settlers with new opportunities to become prosperous. Children of as much as refugees from the 'old corruption' they saw in office achieved by patronage or nepotism access to the security of an official income (Stannage, 1979, 48) and to grants of what turned out in most cases to be worthless land. The very first governor engaged in questionable land dealings (Stannage, 1981, 302), and the gubernatorial power granted in 1837 to appoint to posts worth less than £200 a year was used in accord with 'the custom of the time' i.e. nepotistically (Stannage, 1981, 307). Personal betterment was the motive and the means were not always especially scrupulous, a central theme of not a few interpretations of Australia's political corruption. Reported exceptions deserve note on account of their rarity. It is thus too easy to forget the prevalence of honesty because it was rarely so spectacular in action or consequence as corruption. Only occasionally is it reported, for example in the departure of the wife of Peel, a leading early settler, because of his sharp practice in land survey (Gill, 1962-3, 166). However the *Australian Dictionary of Biography* makes no mention of this. And yet subsequent events and circumstances in the corruption context probably owe less to the early decades of settlement in West Australia than anywhere else in the Australian colonies.

The early periods of European occupance in Victoria and South Australia raise bigger issues, anticipating what followed especially in Victoria. Two strands of political corruption have been discussed in the Victorian case, and emphasised by Kiddle (1961) to the point of centrality in her discussion of pastoralism.[3] In this she first draws attention to English antecedents and to the importance of Vandiemonians and their convict background in the first wave of expansion, and second to the broader environment of the aspiration and ambition to get rich in a difficult environment. In the circumstances of the traditional British constraints on bad behaviour – 'what will the neighbours think?' – were absent. This is not Kiddle ploughing a lonely and eccentric furrow of Victorophobia. It is echoed by other scholars and by contemporary critics. The second strand, less developed by Kiddle, emanates from consideration of the stresses and strains placed on the Victorian public service as population and economic growth accelerated in the 1840s, and the low calibre (and honesty) of many appointees (197). Booth (1869, 81-2) writes of the pre Eureka public service: 'officials were entrusted with the expenditure of a large public revenue who would not have been trusted with the private affairs of any sane man' and whose 'only industry ... was ... in the collection of revenue and its expenditure upon improper objects'. The gold rushes made matters worse, culminating in the incident at Eureka Stockade which was indubitably brought about, at least in the immediate sense, by particular acts of corruption. The magistrate whose behaviour with respect to a murder precipitated the incident was undoubtedly corrupt (Clarke, 743) and the local bureaucracy was made up of friends and relations of the powerful – 'to be made a government official was easy, if one was an officer, of either service, or owned a second cousin distantly related to the aristocracy' (Clarke, 721) – with similar consequences. Carboni (178), an eye witness whose account is generally regarded as among the more reliable, comments: 'the general impression was that "bribery" had smothered the affair (i.e. the murder) in all quarters'. The aftermath did not eliminate corruption from public service, police or goldfields but it did generate decisive reform such as did not occur with respect to land settlement. Most particularly it brought about those legal changes which were one among several reasons why the Australasian goldfields were administered with a reasonable degree of honesty. The existence of sharp practice on the business side is manifest, but government and the political controls of the operational side of the gold industry developed rather differently and to a substantial degree honestly. This is somewhat surprising but well attested, an expression of mateship in tough conditions – recall that the Australian soldier is traditionally a 'digger' – an outcome of good laws sensibly enforced, and perhaps a result of the disparity between what might be got by mining successfully and luckily and what might be got by corrupting the government. If corruption was your game better go for the gullible investor!

South Australia has long enjoyed a reputation as the least corrupt of the Australian states/colonies and equally as the most smugly narrow minded and puritanical. Is this a result of its deliberate and *ab initio* attempt to be different and distinctive (Pike, 1957, 495) or of the respectability of early settlers (43), an outcome of the presence of an unusually large number of non-conformists among the pioneers and their leaders? But recall that the famous non-conformist conscience is a creation more of the second half of the nineteenth century and that like their fellows in all but the convict colonies the first South Australians were after land, profit, and personal advancement. These were just the kind of people the South Australia Company sought to attract and in the process the organisers made what Grenfell Price (1924, 30) deemed the 'fatal mistake of appointing officers who intended to engage in private speculation'. As early as 1846 one squatter summed up the 'sole purpose' of South Australia as 'making money' (Lloyd, 1846, 183), his discussion proceeding along lines similar to those of Kiddle a century later. The colony's first treasurer (Gilles) 'did very well out of land jobbing' (Whitelock, 1977, 24). Low official salaries scarcely helped (Jaensch, 1986, 448). The first decade or so of South Australia was then characterised by extensive official involvement in land, especially urban land, speculation involving even men of the calibre and reputation of Rowland Hill (Pike, 1957, 170). Allegations of sharp practice in this area are common though not all could be regarded as acts of corruption. In one well attested instance a senior official paid for advance information on the quality of land he was considering purchasing (202), and a Colonial Secretary's directive against 'personal interest' was in some cases ignored (173). Tendering involved favouritism (238). Patronage however was from the start an object of public hostility (Pike, 52, 70) though it should be noted that opposition to Lawley's appointment as Governor in 1854 was not just a matter of his being Gladstone's relation but of the fact that he had mishandled public money (475). South Australia could easily have gone the way of the other colonies: the reasons why it to a large degree did not must be left for later discussion.

When the four non-penal colonies are considered not only is the significance of traditional tap roots of the stream of corruption enhanced, usually by overspill and/or descent, but other issues arise, some of them negative but inevitable: the whole ethos and ethics of settlement in a mid-nineteenth century context; and the quality of over-extended governance in a fast growing society and economy. Not everywhere was the result a crisis and response Eureka style but at least in this instance there were positive outcomes. Colonial Australia was to be a creature of many continuities, not least of attitude and outlook. However, representative and responsible colonial government also represented abrupt change and discontinuity.

London ceased to be umpire and became a match referee (without benefit of camera) and power (with all its corrupting propensities) passed quickly to five colonial capitals – their brand new legislatures and well established if sometimes shop soiled judiciaries and administrations, Westminsters in miniature. What was their reputation and record where corruption is concerned?

Notes

1   The great majority of individuals named in chapters three to six are the subject of detailed entries in the *Australian Dictionary of Biography* (*ADB*). At the time of writing the work is complete to 1939 and almost complete for 1940-80 though there are one or two surprising omissions.
2   To judge from media reports abuse of travel and subsistence allowances by members of federal and state legislatures remains widespread.
3   The absence of an index entry under 'corruption' in Kiddle's book is a warning against reading too much into this commonplace phenomenon!

4 'Colonial' Australia

The character of the Australasian political, social and economic order changes dramatically during the middle decades of the nineteenth century, changes highlighted but not delimited by the emergence and evolution of new political institutions. The new order provided a new context and climate for political corruption without presenting a total discontinuity. Thus the most conspicuous change, the end of transportation, did not mean the disappearance of a body of practices and habits – and of course people – inherited from that institutional situation. Australian ways of thinking about government and behaving with respect to it continued and continue to reflect aspects of that formative half century. Thus Finn (1987, 3) refers to 'the enduring attitude which looked to the central government for the satisfaction of needs'. On the other hand key elements of arbitrariness and inequality, universal underpinnings of corruption, had changed, diminished and in some important instances – assignment of convict labour and the corrupt actions of convict clerks – disappeared. Simultaneously the characteristics of immigrants change as well as numbers. The free settlers of mid-century were different in outlook from preceding generations, the children not of Britain's 'old corruption' and poverty but of its new modernisation and prosperity, and a personal ambition which believed that it would fare better in Australia. They sought not grants and patrons to underpin their opportunity but rather the chance to better their condition by taking part in the development of Australia's resources, be it as miner, farmer or trader, in the country or in the town. But as Trollope warned in 1873 (1967, 107), 'The settler, as a matter of course, is in quest of a fortune, and is one who, living among rough things, is apt to become rough and less scrupulous than his dainty brother at home'. Acts of corruption were not to be ruled out in so ambitious a society where everyone aspired to get on – 'what justifications in personal terms of migration were there other than personal success?' (Serle, 1971, 271) – but corruption was not as nearly intrinsic to that success as in the early decades.

Except for the few remaining convicts in general Australia had formally ceased to be an executive-cum-patronage society. Under self-rule patronage did not disappear but it became more and more an internal matter and more and more limited to jobs. (Note however that some authors use the word patronage loosely almost as equivalent to corruption (Trollope, 1967, 480).) While this represented the disappearance of some kinds of corruption it allowed the development of others – the subversion of orderly political process in such mainstream areas as tendering and land settlement. The central element of the situation was the creation of a powerful legislature in each of the colonies, a legislature however by no means separated from the executive function and made up of members evidently, though not exclusively, elected to look after the interests of a particular place and its people, 'the paramountcy of local interest' as Quaife (1969, 54) describes it. These new members possessed patronage in the narrow sense, but more importantly they had power – votes, influence, access to decision makers, information – which could be used corruptly. The extent to which certain kinds of use of these powers might reasonably be described as corrupt is as already noted an important and difficult issue. A geographical element is introduced by reiterating the fact that members were elected to perform not only a broader public duty – to defend (colonial) public interest – but also a narrower local one, broadly coincident with their electorate.

The Australia of colonial self-rule, approximately the second half of the nineteenth century, represented also a different political geography, that of six colonies. Given that by mid-century all, with the exception of Western Australia, were entering a period of rapid economic and social change, it is scarcely surprising that the succeeding half century, even while the colonies discussed the idea of a Commonwealth, is a period when intercolonial diversity is at its greatest. Australia must at this period perforce be discussed as six rather than one, even though there is no absence of common themes and experiences.

Tasmania and South Australia

In two of the colonies the most significant characteristic is the apparently low incidence of political corruption. There the parallel ends, for Tasmania and South Australia contribute to our understanding of the issues in quite different ways. The modest presence in Tasmania is the simple product of modest levels of development. Tasmania's only recorded boom was over and a larger proportion of land and resources had been appropriated than elsewhere in Australia before mid-century. What corruption occurred was essentially a continuation of the old tradition. The 1840s, the last convict decade, had been characterised by 'officials sometimes given to venal conduct' (Townley, 1991, 47). Things may not have been as bad as a generation earlier, but could scarcely yet be described as good. In the colonial period, for example, a corrupt surveyor's obvious acquisitiveness (and eventual dismissal, only to take up a parliamentary career!) in terms of fraud and evasion of the land regulations could enable him to more than double his own land holdings in twenty years (Denholm, 1980, 191-3). This was small beer by mainland standards, like most of the rest of colonial Tasmania's corruption. One interpretation also suggests the significance of a much larger convict presence in the island than elsewhere in Australia, but more in terms of élite reaction, 'defence of moral standards' and at worst 'snobbery and punctiliousness' than of actual corruption (Reynolds, 1969, 26). The 1890s generated suspicion of corruption in a major bank failure which could not be eliminated by carefully restricting the terms of reference of a Royal Commission (Robson, 2, 175); and in the activities of several ministers in for example, railways, lands, mines and public works (Robson, 2, 180-1). More generally ministerial misconduct and the behaviour of 'roads and bridges' members are a microcosm of a broader experience better explored in richer and fuller form elsewhere. In corruption as more generally the island retreats to the margins of Australia's history and geography from mid century, already substantially developed, set in its ways (a modest but perceptible degree of corruption included) and usually forgotten by its neighbours.

South Australia was also a small and isolated colony but with a maybe overstated reputation for political cleanliness (an offshoot of its godliness) which has been sustained. Its nineteenth century experience is again in one sense insignificant when compared to the south-eastern colonies, but it is also exemplary and even a working counterfactual. What made South Australia different? Certainly land speculation had been a central and widespread and corrupt activity in the early period (Price, 1924, 167 and 238-9) and land remained the objective of most settlers. On one view land speculators dominated the first twenty years of the colony's parliament (Bowes, 1968, 94). Note however that urban land dominated this sphere of action in the early period, and that while South Australia had a squattocracy it also had a large and accessible area of land clearly suitable in every respect (debate as to its margins excepted) for arable farming. The public service early acquired (Jaensch, 1986, 155; Hawker, 1979, 57) and sustained a reputation for honesty in which it received public support (Jaensch, 453) if not great public esteem or high salaries. Twopenny's favourable 1883 assessment (1863, 161) may have reflected absence of need as much as higher standards of probity. A vestigial Wakefieldism emphasised orderly process in the area of land sales. Finally and famously Torrens, in legislation passed in 1858, gave South Australia a system of land transfer and registration applicable to the somewhat confused *status quo* and which despite predictable opposition from lawyers proved to be so satisfactory as to be widely emulated. In Goyder (Surveyor-General 1861-94) it possessed an impeccably honest senior public servant in a key role. This is not to say there was no corruption: an 1865 select committee (South Australia, 1865, ii-v and Q 686-7 and 2380-2) heard evidence of bribery of and by members, clerks and land agents; Bowes (1968, 222) notes that a land agent MP was expelled for bribe taking in 1877 and the same historian remarks (231) that the orderly settlement scene of the 1870s owes as much to sometimes questionable action by parliamentarians as to good law. Even land reformers (Ward for example) were corruptible when their own personal affairs were in disarray (Hirst, 1973, 112-3). By 1890 a report on the disposal of Crown Lands (South Australia, 1890) was generally favourable.

Credit must to Goyder and Torrens (Stein, 1981) but the latter remains in the eyes of some a controversial figure. His broader importance cannot be gainsaid and is well stated in most works of reference: his less well known critics aver that as landowners on the basis of a generation of jobbing and some inside information the Torrens family and their like stood to gain hugely from reform of the process of land registration and transfer which would lock in their ill gotten gains (Jaensch, 1986, 159-61; Borrow, 1984). Conflict of interest inevitably rears its ambiguous head in a small society where the able and ambitious had very wide ranging bus.ness interests. As Bowes comments 'how intricately woven together was public interest and private gain in the thinking and legislative activity of parliamentarians' (180). Most such situations represented not two conflicting interests – public and private – but a complex set of such, exercises in the sharp distinction of which would have been not merely intellectually taxing but a recipe for standstill, and not merely in South Australia. On a longer and broader view Torrens served the wider interests of the community and anyone who does so opens himself to accusations of corruption as long as judgements are based on an ethic which focuses on narrow – and in practice impossible – distinctions rather than on situations in context. Everyone and everywhere gains from the practical resolution of a long standing muddle.

Queensland

There is certainly little ambiguity as to the role of corruption in land settlement in colonial Queensland except perhaps in the minds of some of those who have written on the subject. It can only be described as endemic and deep seated, a reflexion less of particularly difficult problems – there was for example little legacy from the first half of the nineteenth century to sort out – than of an ethos of development, an atmosphere of class war, and the personality of key players.

One of the best and best known studies of all land settlement in the colonial period, Waterson (1968) on the Darling Downs, leaves the reader in little doubt as to the importance of corruption. Waterson places the emphasis, I think accurately, not upon direct bribery but upon many different varieties of favouritism exercised in favour of the pastoral interest against the small farmer or would be farmer (33-4). Note that Waterson this early in his work conceded their political defensibility. Neither politicians nor officials were inclined to enforce the law as to leasehold conditions (35), dummying, and false declarations (40-1). Advance warning was given to squatters when their occupance was threatened (40). Land was viewed not as a trust but as a mere commodity (116). (It is also interesting to note that the 1873 Municipal Contracts Act which sought to regulate members' activity in the area of contracts excluded land (Bernays, 1919, 343).) In 1870 Taylor, Lands Minister, 'gazetted resumptions to suit himself and his friends' (Waterson, 1968, 35). In the Kennedy District of North Queensland Allingham (1977, 26) records that the coming into force of new land legislation on 1 January 1861 was marked by the Land Commissioner with a Hogmanay Party for 'a rather select group of his former exploration companions'. In the early hours of New Year's Day one of them put in the first registered run application. She goes on to observe, 'in (thus) using his official position ... not breaking the law ... contrary to present day ideas of the moral responsibility of those in public office ... conduct like this was quite common'. Nevertheless it was on most views corrupt. She is not however of the view that corruption underlay the Act's failure to discourage speculative occupance which she ascribes rather to an understaffed public service (42-8). In such a context Epps's (1894, 86-102) comment that Queensland had few problems in this area makes no sense at all even by comparison with his more extended treatment of New South Wales.

Given the extent of the problem the wide range of suggested causes is no surprise. Queensland's public service was not renowned for its honesty (Waterson, 1968, 33-4) – much of the corruption required its collusion – or in the case of lands its organisation. Patronage and influence did not in this context serve the colony well. Nor did rather insecure conditions of employment. The dominant figure in the public service Gregory was a notable explorer but a poor organiser. The *Australian Dictionary of*

Biography describes him as 'personally incorruptible' (without interpreting the phrase) while recognising that he blatantly favoured squatters, was lax and secretive as an administrator and willing to condone abuses. MacIntyre (1985, 36) proffers cheap land as a cause, a perspective upon the situation in which politicians set and worked the rules of a process pitting widespread popular demand against entrenched class power – shades of old England! He goes on to note that every Lands Minister in the colony's first fifteen years lost some of his good reputation. Moorehead (premier in 1882) was alleged to take 2.5% on Crown lands sales (Murphy, 1978, 101-2). McIlwraith, the most corrupt of all Queensland's colonial premiers used Queensland National Bank funds, and as one of its promoters he secured the government account for the bank, in order to speculate in land (Taylor, 1967, 81-5; Murphy, 101-3). In this period (and beyond) development was the central issue and gained a paramountcy it has never lost, an ethos and determination intrinsic to the settlement process but carried to extremes in this particular case. This extreme, where individual gain is esteemed above not only public good and process of law but any sense of social justice, has been ascribed by some commentators to the Scots origins of several key figures (Murphy and Joyce, 1978, 127). The Scots were not peculiarly dominant in Queensland but the particularities of timing and personality may go some way to support this thesis, a particular and unattractive manifestation of those attributes which more generally made Scots such successful colonists. For in this period Queensland's 'develop and be damned' ethos comes into existence (Fitzgerald, 1982, 114-5). Scotland at its rare worst was Queensland's misfortune, just as South Australia eventually benefited from the favourable components of England's Nonconformist conscience. Finally Allingham's comment (1977, 26) on the practical difficulty encountered by the press in its watchdog role, in essence a problem of great distances, deserves reiteration.

Land is simply the best known, as yet most fully and easily explored, dimension of Queensland's culture of political corruption during the second half of the nineteenth century, a culture established early and then at least in general terms in receipt of more public support than criticism. That corruption extended predictably to railways, to their routes and to associated contracts, and thus to public works more generally. A Municipal Contracts Act in 1873 (Bernays, 1919, 393) perhaps clipped the local politicians' wings a little, in response to a Speaker's ruling in 1869 which favoured the member with any but a very direct interest (Waterson, 1968, 31). *Ad hoc* authorities also met with anti corruption success at the municipal level (Laverty, 277). Taylor (1967, 85) argues that in all this the political elite used their power to further their own business interests but without going so far as to shape policy for this end, a somewhat academic distinction. Certainly the propensity towards distinguishing public and private interests was absent (Taylor, 81), but recall that in a miniscule colonial world where a small group had extensive commercial interests integral to the progress of the colony (as well as lots of relations) to debar them from the political process would have been to deprive government of much needed talent. In any event it must be pointed out that Queensland was not without political participants of proven probity. Lilley (Murphy and Joyce, 1978, 91), Kidston (*ibid.*, 202) and Macrossan (*ibid.*, 107) (who left the ministry to avoid a conflict of interest) provide three significant examples. There were also occasionally positive actions, against dummying in 1874-5 (Waterson, 1968, 43-4) but they stand out as exceptional. More typically, as with the Peak Downs land scales scandal in 1882, there were accusations but enquiries got nowhere (Fitzgerald, 1982, 314-5).

Lastly Queensland throws light on the obscure topic of the day to day methods of the corrupt businessmen, an area successfully tracked down more often by the workings of chance than by sophisticated methods of enquiry. An enquiry into public works in 1900 (Queensland, 1900, Q 9197) explains how well connected builders and others got tender information from the Public Works Department and acted corruptly on it. Telegraph tenders were accepted for some time after the official (mail delivery related) time closure: all that was needed was a friendly, well placed, and well rewarded clerk with access to a telephone and the most competitive tender could be undercut. Interestingly this gem of practical information is unindexed in an otherwise well indexed report: too trivial; already widely known; too sensitive? Interestingly too the final report does not take up this issue: again one wonders why.

The overall situation in Queensland may then be summed up as driven by personally ambitious settlers with a limited concept of conflict of interest, a public opinion unwilling to press home complaint or enquiry in instances where by any reasonable standard or definition there had been corruption, and a compliant and not particularly efficient public service. Colonial Queensland's development process was replete with corruption. Its exact dimensions are unknown and unknowable although there is plenty of scope for further case studies, inexact though their conclusions will certainly be. Even suspicions might be counted, the pastoral leases held onto in doubtful circumstances for example. And there are the more precise cases, for example the difference between McIlwraith's price and the market price for steel rails. Exploration of the extra costs which corruption represented and the different geographies to which it contributed, not a reductionist account with corruption centre stage, is the agenda for further study. Finally, Taylor's explanation of the diminution from late in the century of political corruption of this kind – manifestly not the disappearance of the phenomenon – in terms of external control, economic expansion, party government and a stronger state, deserves reiteration (Taylor, 1967, 92).

Land

Contextual Issues

Queensland was a fast growing colony. Even so it remained marginal to the south-eastern heartland, devoid not only of the dimension of preceding history, so powerful in New South Wales, but also of the strong urban component – in brief Sydney and Melbourne – to be set alongside the rural. Queensland remained a distant place-getter behind the two colonial thoroughbreds. And thoroughbreds they certainly were, transformed in half a century from the pioneer and penal periphery to wealth rivalled globally, at least on a per capita basis, in very few other places. Melbourne in particular was the epitome of such quick-fire success. Where did political corruption fit into that process?

As to the political process the apparatus of government in each of these colonies (as in the other three) comprised a bicameral legislature charged to provide laws to supplement the existing and inherited frameworks. Its formal constraints comprised not a written constitution but gubernatorial power to refer certain kinds of legislation to London and, more significantly in our context, paucity of political and administrative resources. There was, especially in New South Wales, an inherited administrative tradition with a strong element, reform attempts notwithstanding, of patronage. Patronage was both initially under attack – Trollope called it the curse of the colonies (1967, 185) – and yet also alive and well, with a tendency to bounce back after exercises in reform in the last decades of the century.

Members were at first unpaid and legislative sessions were therefore short. Colonial government was primarily a matter of the day to day exercise of administrative and political functions by ministers and public servants to develop and increase resources – land, minerals, infrastructure, immigration. Even as legislators and for a larger part of the year when they were not in session, members (including ministers) were also local lobbyists, seeking to ensure that their district (and political base) received a fair (or preferably more than fair) go in the development of its resources and the disbursement of public money. The colonial governments were necessarily activist, driven by the imperative of development they were impelled 'into activities without counterpart in Britain' (Finn, 1987, 40).

The legislators' role was enhanced by two further factors, the almost non-existence of local government outside the two metropoles and other large towns. The colonial government was the *de facto* local government, and weak party organisation allowed the member – arguably corruptly – to align his parliamentary role very closely to the interests of his electorate. For rural members one key part of that interest was land alienation, an interest shared in and controlled by a government to which it was a key resource, both fiscal and political. It was also an area of conflict, not only ideological and intellectual, but personal and class, where an established élite of large scale pastoralists – squatters – competed with actual or prospective smaller farmers – settlers – for a resource which was fragile and poorly understood and which in terms of intrinsic attributes favoured sometimes one group, sometimes the other – and often neither.

In this context the New South Wales 1888 Centennial History which provides a short sketch of each Member of the House of Representatives provides both an interesting antidote to exaggeration and an insight into contemporary attitudes. It is by no means bland, but only one member is singled out for critical comment – 'personal aggrandisement appears to be the cause of his enthusiasm' (Morrison, 1888, 2, 548). Members in what might be deemed suspect activities – notably land speculators and also auctioneers – are not so condemned. To what extent is this evaluation a matter of contemporary attitudes different from ours, to what extent a recognition that only thoroughly bad eggs were deemed corrupt, were known as such, and were few? All the evidence suggests that colonial society had a higher threshold of tolerance of corruption than exists at the end of the twentieth century although of course there was great individual variation. Corrupt individuals were viewed with less hostility than the system as a whole. Practices with similar outcomes were not judged identically: thus inside information was used for personal gain with very little disapproval whereas direct bribery was regarded more seriously. However this may be a reflexion of context. Land alienation, or rather its obstruction in the squatter interest, commonly enough generated bribery, but the relatively low tolerance of bribery – when, usually with difficulty, the offender could be caught and the offence proved – probably reflected the hostility of the many who were thereby losers against wealthy few who gained. Squatters certainly appear in an unattractive light as do many surveyors (Walker, 1958, 70), both those in the public service and those on contract, and a minority of public servants in general. The point that in this area corruption needed the cooperation of several parties, not all necessarily equally guilty, should also be noted. Members and their supporters seeking rewards were also intrinsically more conspicuous in the case of public works, of railways, roads and bridges, than in the area of lands. But in both instances the idea of the public interest if never quite forgotten was rarely as vigorously pursued as its private counterpart. The various forms of 'roads and bridges' corruption were made the more acceptable by the 'progressive' character of what they achieved – and in the end almost everyone got something – as opposed to the obstructionism which motivated much of the corruption in the land business.

Land: New South Wales

New South Wales' longer experience of the processes of land alienation in circumstances of extreme environmental diversity had not been a fortunate one. In the last decades of the nineteenth century the outcomes and procedures of a century were almost universally condemned, and that condemnation pointed a finger at corruption. Among Australian examples Adams (1893, 199) points to 'stupidity and corruption' as central to what he regarded as failure to solve 'the one essentially real Australian Question – the Land Question', and in the same year Ranken entitled a book on the subject, extensively quoted by Epps (1894, 14 and 23), *Our Wasted Heritage* in which he attributes the bad results of 1847 land legislation to official abuse. Among visitors Dilke in 1868 and 1890, by when he saw improvement, and the widely read and travelled Trollope agreed. Dilke (1868, 1, 40) tellingly observed that in a single generation the squatter's status had shifted from lawbreaker to nabob (still then understood as a byword for ill gotten gain). Trollope focuses upon the strong albeit occasional element of breach of trust in the forms of favouritism and influence 'as though the only principle upon which it was possible to act – that of the land being in truth the property of the colonists who would go and use it – had been forgotten, thrown over and abandoned' (1967, 274). If blame is to be apportioned it appears to reside at the middle level, in members and land occupiers – persons of substance in the community – bringing pressure to bear on often willing public servants (and occasionally dissentient members of their own class) in their own interest. One particular instance, evidently widespread, was advance access to information. A reminiscent clergyman quotes a member's remark, 'I knew what was coming – I have sold out' and describes his demeanour not as guilty but as self-congratulatory ('A Clergyman', 1894, 11). The same source reports that in New England a government official made £7000 'dabbling in lots put in his hand by the government for sale' ('A Clergyman', 1894, 297). A good, if not necessarily typical, example of a successful middle level operator is Pratt, a Sydney schoolmaster who used corrupt methods, personal connexions, hospitality and the telegraph. His personal circumstance – the advantages of city residence where legal access to relevant maps and documents was easier and marginally but significantly earlier, and his own intellectual skills as a Cambridge educated mathematician – enhanced his ability successfully to defend and expand his land interests (Coward, 1969, 35-79). Squatters certainly bribed surveyors to protect their occupance. Baker (1958, 70) notes a (Queensland) case at Bundamba Lagoon Ipswich where farms were surveyed around the lagoon but had no road access except over the pastoral holding. But squatters could also be victims: J.H. Broughton was allegedly deprived of his run because he was the Premier's son's electoral opponent ('A Clergyman', 1868, 280). Surveyors also often acted corruptly on their own initiative with a view to the future of their private practice abusing their authority under the 1861 legislation to 'block any application which, in their opinion, interfered with the interests of the public estate' (Robinson, 1976, 63). On one view (Gammage, 1990, 117 and 121) the structures of New South Wales land law during the period 1860-90, and even more strongly the failure to make amendments where experience had shown up deficiencies which facilitated corruption, come close to supporting a conspiratorial interpretation. Gammage simultaneously argues the need for detailed local study, a case eminently supportable in the corruption context.

Towards the end of the century the situation improved. There was some degree of decentralisation and depoliticisation (Epps, 1874, 39). Comment along these lines appears in Dilke's later work (1890, 2, 229), in Epps (1894, 39), and in Walker (1958, 70). The 1883 report which highlighted the outcomes of the 1861 legislation (an 'unintelligible chaos' (New South Wales, 1883, 15)) was in part responsible, exposing a situation in which 'as the law became more intricate and involved ministerial patronage and Parliamentary interest became more frequent' (*ibid.*, 15); 'conservation and beneficial management ... the last matters considered' (*ibid.*, 29); 'the most effective mode of getting business done at the "lands" a land agent who is a member of the popular branch'. Robinson (1976, 72) neatly juxtaposes Buxton's (Riverina) comments (1967, 72) as to 'perjury, immorality, corruption and violence' with the observation that the settlement process nevertheless proceeded. Quantification and precision in this context is as yet generally unachieved. It is possible up to a point in principle, but at the cost of great archival labour rather out of fashion in contemporary research. The probability is that it would vindicate Dilke, Epps and Walker despite the fact of great land scandals at ministerial level in the first decade of the twentieth century. The activities of a succession of crooks – notably Crick and Willis – who required bribes to act or more often to act expeditiously and in partisan fashion in particular policy areas are exceptionally well documented in a Royal Commission report of monumental size and magisterial authority. Its fascination lies also in the chairman's struggle to assert his authority against participants who had made a great deal of money but had also left a careless paper trail and a supply of hostile witnesses. It should not be read as evidence for the apogee of rottenness, though Epps' overall verdict in 1894 (50) was that progress notwithstanding, New South Wales land laws remained 'a monument of muddle' (1894), an example of thoroughly and persistently bad barrels containing not a few bad apples.

Victoria

In the broadest terms the Victorian situation was not greatly different from that of New South Wales. If there was no direct continuum from the convict period yet there was a continuous substratum of corruption varying in thickness and never quite to disappear. Booth (1869), one time Inspector of Settlements to the Government of Victoria, presents a particularly cogent and detailed account with an understandably strong focus on land issues for the 1850s and 1860s. The elements are familiar: action by ministers and members in their own and their friends' and supporters' interests, inside information, bribery, a high but variable degree of public tolerance, often ill-conceived legislation implemented by a public service of uneven quality.

Potential case studies abound. Consider for example the allegations against C.E. Jones, Railways Minister and MP for Ballarat, in 1869 (Bate, 1978, 142). He was allegedly paid by Hugh Glass, a millionaire squatter, to soften the 1869 Lands Bill. A contemporary historian regarded Jones as 'no worse than many who had gone unpunished' and this in a city where standards were relatively high. Glass's organisation spent £80000 (*ADB*) – lobbying or bribing? He was found guilty of corrupt practice in 1869 but the decision was reversed on appeal. 'The popularity of his release derived as much from the feeling that parliament was corrupt ... as from any sympathy with Glass.' (*ADB*). Once more individuals are more reluctantly blamed than institutions. McQuilton's study of Ned Kelly discusses the ways in which squatters corruptly abused the system in North Eastern Victoria in the 1860s and 1870s (McQuilton, 1979, 34-8). By contrast his account of the police is emphatically one of incompetence though the official enquiry into the incident did find that the Detective Branch was riddled with corruption (180).

Surveyors were as always well placed, Wright (1989, 121) noting that their poor reputation based on their substantial powers of discretion was substantially deserved goes on to remark 'that it is difficult to determine the extent of the corruption', but also that reputation notwithstanding, most were reasonably honest. He further notes (130) the reputation of Ligar (Surveyor General in 1862) for shady dealing. This kind of reputation goes back as far as Victoria's first Surveyor-General, Hoddle (Turner, 1-211). Bribery is commonplace in the evidence given before the Crown Lands Commission in 1878-9 (Powell, 1973, xxxii-xxxiii) but Powell's emphasis is upon the general 'combination of ignorance and venality' and he advises against the futility of isolating individuals.

Among writers on rural Victoria Kiddle (1961) deserves special note in this context because of her concern with and extended discussion – a generation ahead of its time - of settler morality, a morality she regarded as weakened both by its penal connexions (Kiddle, 26) and by even the process of free emigration quoting Backhouse (1843): 'when they emigrate to a country where this (i.e. neighbours' oversight) is withdrawn, too generally but little that has the appearance of principle remains' (*ibid.*, 103). And yet 'these Presbyterians honestly believed themselves God's chosen ... it was not long before worldly prosperity, the symbol of virtue, became of over-mastering importance' (*ibid.*, 130). The quest for prosperity tends to corrupt and in Kiddle's view (*ibid.*, 131) was passed down from generation to generation. The chapter on Duffy's 1862 Land Act (*ibid.*, 233-62) is entitled 'A Simple System of Corruption'; the act's third section examines 'bribery, corruption, false-swearing and similar practices' (*ibid.*, 236). Successful legislation arrived only after the squatters had won the day. Significantly she ascribed the same effects to inefficient administration (*ibid.*, 267) as to corruption, formally warning against over emphasis of the latter. But the work as a whole endorses corruption's centrality, while admiring the pioneers' tenacity.

West Australia

West Australia is the most anomalous among the six colonies in terms of both broad political experience and the more particular issue of corruption. Representative government and the development surge came only at the end of the century, convictism and the apparatus of the convict order – a commissariat, blatant nepotism – continued well into the second half of the nineteenth century. Hampton, governor 1862-9, brought with him from Tasmania a reputation for corruption and nepotism which he did nothing to diminish (Stannage, 1981, 302). It is of interest to note that such a man could be so appointed as late as the 1860s, even to a backwater. It must be added however that while some officials tried to enrich themselves in the early decades along lines similar to those pursued more successfully and centrally in New South Wales and Tasmania, the Western Australian commissariat never performed a similar role to that of its counterparts (Statham, 1984). As to land, the *raison d'être* of the settlement, accusations of corruption can be and were levelled against the surveyors who used advance information to amass large estates, at least until regulations were tightened in 1880, but the actual situation was one of land of very low value and of an almost non-existent market: corruption of a very long-term and almost nominal character (Crowley, 1971, 100-7). Trollope's view was that corruption in Western Australia in the form of nepotism was inevitable with so small a population (1967, 594-5), but he does not discuss the broader problems of very slow development and convict origins (342) at least in terms of corruption (342, 594-5). The closest resemblance to the other colonies in the domain of corruption was at the infrastructural and municipal level most obviously so in Perth but this is to anticipate examination of a new set of issues.

Nowhere in colonial Australia was the operation of the land market a clear and clean administrative process. 'Influence at the lands office' (Roberts, 1924, 4) was widespread. In Victoria and New South Wales it was a central part of the process, but never it must at once be added the whole. Most of the colonies managed to complicate the essentially simple process of getting people on to the land, a legislative and administrative situation on and in which medium corruption thrived. 'Corruption was endemic extending from the humblest licensed surveyor to the most permanent senior official and his Minister ... land agents with plentiful funds and accomplices in the civil service' is MacIntyre's description and assessment (1985, 36). Land agents appear to have been an especially pernicious force. The mess may in turn be traced back to the confused inheritance of the convict period and the limited foresight of British officials when settlement was first proposed and planned. Its other significant element, again with early roots and a continuing momentum, was competition for land, apparent abundance notwithstanding, between a small, powerful and well established group who had early seized the opportunity to establish themselves on a large scale but with a rather uncertain title – the squattocracy – and a larger group of actual and would be farmers – the settlers – who sought to use their numbers and their growing political power to gain legally secure rural occupance. Bribery and corruption in a variety of forms thus became weapons of class war in a situation exacerbated by the peculiarities of prior history and an unfamiliar environment. It required men and measures of unusual vision and vigour to minimise this situation, and only in one Australian colony was this early the case. Most of Australia had to live with the burden of corruption in this area through most of the period of primary European occupance and the momentum of the phenomenon appears to have carried forward into both the land-use planning process of the second half of the twentieth century and into attitudes in general. It must also be recalled that environmental conditions favoured extensive pastoral occupance over a much wider area of Australia than would have suited most settlers and not a few politicians: the corrupt pastoralist was not infrequently doing the 'right deed for the wrong reason',[1] and by dishonest means. Finally a connexion between land sales and 'roads and bridges' expenditure, now rarely commented upon but noted at the time, should be mentioned. *The Express* 16 December 1882 (King, 1957, 79) remarks: 'land sales have filled the Treasury and the full Treasury has enabled nearly every electorate and nearly every representative to be bought by a lavish local expenditure'. Land sales were not only subject to corruption *per se* but funded its other manifestations.

Infrastructure and Public Works

Land is not the whole colonial tale. Attention must now be turned to a range of other issues, to infrastructure and public works – railways in particular – to the cities as well as the countryside, and to a political context which renders the concept of political corruption even more difficult.

The most spectacular infrastructures of colonial Australia and the most thoroughly controlled by the colonial governments were the railways. They were also the most popular – a political panacea – the most expensive, and seemingly the most durable. They extended across a spectrum from lines destined to link colonial capitals, through those opening up rural and provincial areas, to suburban lines and tramways. In terms of propensity to corruption, at least in the planning and construction stage, it is the second and third of these that matter most. In the first category routes and priorities almost determined themselves, and so one area of decision where elsewhere corruption was widely prevalent is diminished. But when it comes to the later phase of secondary, branch and suburban lines there was intense competition to obtain a line – 'local expectations' in Trollope's understated phrase (1967, 268-9) – a matter of life and death for existing communities and of both windfall and ongoing profits for landowners. This is the basis of Meudell's distinction (1929, 216) between a sensible early phase of railway building and the later phase of 'political railways'. There is every reason to believe that various forms of corruption were extensively used to gain and to exploit the advantage of a railway, by means such as bribes, inside information, and several forms of political influence. Coghlan (1918, 1419-20) describes the process as 'a scramble ... for as much local expenditure as they (MPs) could secure': Adams (1893, 191) the end result thus: 'railways have a habit of running into the properties of millionaires, despite all local agitations to the contrary, and considering the enormous sums realised by such courses it is not surprising that average members of the Assembly have frequently (especially in 'the old days') found their banking accounts liable to sudden expansion'. Note here: firstly corruption flying in the face of local and probably well informed opinion, secondly the role of the 'average members', and thirdly some acknowledgment even by a radical critic that things had got better. As a purely rational exercise pursued by honest process Australia's railway development would have had a different outcome, and one can envisage an interesting if hypothetical counterfactual exercise and comparison, even if one suspects that the result would have been less different from actuality, at least in broad terms and especially in rural areas, than has at times been suggested. But Australia was in a hurry: everywhere wanted a railway – now! Parkes' New South Wales Railway Commission (Parkes, 1892, 201-2 and 391-2), while not primarily an attempt to slow down approval, did aim to connect ministerial responsibility and parliamentary authority via that detailed investigation which the corrupt so wished to avoid.

In any event a number of questions have to be asked and placed into context. Was the member who used influence as well as argument to press for a railway to pass through a district which he represented behaving corruptly? What if he used his vote in general support of the ministry in return for that particular end in a parliament of faction rather than party? What of the fact that in most instances the member would own land and have wider business interests in the area which he was serving to benefit? And in some cases he might be interested in several communities and districts which were competing for a railway or a bridge. Not only was the expected role of the member, which unfulfilled would lead to personal, local, or even regional disaster, one which was open to a corrupt interpretation, but its limits were unclearly laid down by law and/or custom and in some respects – notably the use of insider information for personal gain – set as has been noted at limits which would now be regarded as unacceptable by a very wide margin. Corruption of process was not simply a matter of votes. At least one case of mysterious disappearance of an official report occurred in New South Wales (Fitzgerald, 1987, 68).

It may not have been the most rational way to develop a railway system, it may not have been entirely free of corruption, but it is easy to overstate corruption's role and significance in this general context. (One scholar, Frost, in the rural Victorian case, does offer an almost corruption free if not totally convincing interpretation (1986).) When all that has been said the presence of corruption is scarcely to be gainsaid, but it is to be looked at not only at the grand political scale of line planning but also in the more local details of safety (Twopenny, 1883, 154) and station location (Cannon, 1966, 31). On this basis too country railways were less the domain of corruption than their suburban counterparts, an evaluation complicated as well as clarified by the existence of in depth studies of the latter in Melbourne (Cannon, 1966).

In the suburbs, of Melbourne in particular, urban growth both necessitated and generated railway and tramway development so that the rapidly growing city workforce could be housed. The constraints here were not environmental but of distance: virtually all land within a certain distance, as fixed at any particular time by technological factors, was ripe for suburban growth if it had a railway or tramway. The political decision as to where these ran, as to where and when suburbs developed, was up for grabs and undoubtedly corrupt. Members sold influence, information and votes, landowners were keen buyers. The situation was well publicised at the time: the subject of satirical verse in the *Argus* it is treated in a fashion which clearly assumes widespread public interest and knowledge (Davidson, 1970, 179). The story has been retold by Cannon (1966), and as told by him has been criticised, less however in terms of substance and detail than in terms of eventual outcome (Serle, 1971, 81, 262). After all, in the medium term Melbourne gained an enviable public transport system, though in the short run it was over extended and expensive. Cannon's study is set in a wider context which arguably opens him to such criticism. He himself would recognise that the devil of corruption in Melbourne's case lay as already noted in the detail, in the location of stations and the preparation of timetables (Serle, 1971, 265-6). At this point Melbourne's general reputation for a 'low condition of commercial morality' (Boehm, 1971, 267) in the 1890s, whether or not worse than elsewhere in the continent, is scarcely to be doubted and has been ascribed a role in the city's fall from Australian financial leadership (Boehm, 1971, 267). At the other extreme the building of South Australia's railways, at least as thoroughly explored by Meinig (1962, chapter 7), appears to have been almost corruption free. For this the personality and reputation of Surveyor

General Goyder and the procedures employed appear primarily responsible. This was South Australia's great good fortune given the importance and railway dependence of its wheat export trade.

On the longest view then the issue of corruption and the colonial railways becomes not one of unnecessary lines to inappropriate places, but of the cost of construction and the conditions of operation, safety included. Both of these adverse factors long hung over the state systems. But they also provided instances of false accusation by powerful opponents, in New South Wales in the early 1890s for example (New South Wales, 1892). As to suburban transport again the burden of cost argument applies, and the overall shapes of networks were affected to the point that even in the golden age some lines were quickly abandoned. Corruption was conspicuously irrational. The money that went via corruption into private pockets was an extra cost for an initially inferior system to say nothing of ongoing operational expenditure.

Railways and tramways were the sharpest end of the larger and blunter developmental instrument of public works, an instrument by definition political, exceptionally but not as we shall see exclusively concentrated at the level of colonial government, and extremely vulnerable to corruption. The essence of this situation is expressed in the contemporary expression 'roads and bridges' member: roads and bridges were another region of the heartland of colonial politics, perpetual and universal, less costly and less spectacular than railways, but a domain calling for and providing a constant stream of decisions and expenditures. The duty of the 'roads and bridges' member, especially in the eyes of the electorate, was to get this money spent in his electorate, both for the immediate cash flow and the assumed, not always real, long term benefit, rather than elsewhere. He must get more than a fair share, and the usual means to this end was voting support in the house. On this basis an intrinsic and greater corruption in the early factional period of colonial politics has been alleged over the emergent party form (Loveday and Martin, 1966). Parkes himself acted thus in 1868 for a bridge and a wharf (Loveday and Martin, 1966, 96). Two decades later, in a leadership role, his attitude, expressed in the 1887 Public Works Bill (Parkes, 1892, 150 and 191) had changed.

Whether this kind of suspension of common sense and critical faculty was truly corrupt rather than a short-lived phase in the emergence of a party focused stability is open to question. If pork barrel politics be corrupt – on today's consensus it is – then it is alive and well in the Australian states and can be traced back into the colonial period. What is more clearly corrupt, and was and is less explored and less publicised, is a range of corrupt practices in the execution of public works (Sheldon, 1993, 54) – in essence not giving the job to the best firm because either another has bribed, or on the basis of favouritism of a political or personal character. Roads might not only be corruptly located, they might be unduly expensive to make and maintain, which returns us to the cost of corruption, the shrinking of governmental capacity to do public things because private interests got more than their efforts or merits deserved. Western Australia provides interesting examples, albeit just into the Commonwealth period, in the domain of water supply both for Coolgardie and Perth, as well as a strikingly *avant garde* interpretation of their implications (West Australia, 1902 (1 and 2)). In the Coolgardie case the contractor and engineer enjoyed an unacceptably close relationship and the latter acquired valuable land in advance. Likewise the manager of Perth Waterworks employed friends and relations. What is striking for an age which so often saw corruption in resigned or victimless terms is the reaction of the official enquiries: 'every shilling of unnecessary expenditure ... represents an illegitimate burden on the population using the water' (West Australia, 1902 (1), xx) and 'Perth would, in our opinion, have had a better potable supply of fresh water today' (West Australia, 1902 (2), 5). Corruption represents a cost and makes a difference.

Cities and Towns

A present day observer of Australian society and politics will soon encounter both reality and mythology of bribery and corruption in the domain of public works, as well as its discussion in terms similar to those enshrined in the Royal Commissions of a century ago. However in that colonial period as now Australia was a continent where central (colonial) government was unusually strong and continuous, real local government weak and often discontinuous especially in the cities and larger towns. (In the rural areas it scarcely existed.) This is one reason why it is a relatively underdiscussed and as yet largely inaccessible topic except at the metropolitan level where professional historians have been at work.

When that has been said it remains the case that Australia's great cities are the subject of excellent historical scholarship at a variety of scales which exposes – even revels in – the extent of political corruption. In at least one case it is the focal point. Elsewhere judgement remains suspended even as suspicions are strong. Fitzgerald (1987 and 1992), Barrett (1971 and 1979), Dunstan (1984) and Stannage (1981) leave the reader in no doubt as to the extent and significance of political corruption in three of Australia's metropoles in the colonial half century, nor for that matter of the arbitrary character of that cut off date. The municipal strand is arguably the most continuous of all in Australia's political corruption. To list its components is, at the risk of tedium, to cover the whole of local government. Thus in Sydney Fitzgerald (1992) mentions *inter alia* markets (62), water supply (77-8) (gratuities to inspectors, favoured treatment of councillors and their property), labour hiring (157-61) and slum housing (1987, 68) though she also comments on the unreality of much of the public criticism of the 1840s and 1850s (50). In some of these examples the essentially ideological defence is entered, that some of these – labour hiring practices for example – were no more than a proletarian parallel to opportunities taken (less controversially) by businessmen councillors in their own interest (157-61). Larcombe's emphasis is rather upon bad legislation, inferior and unqualified men at all levels, low salaries and inadequate audit (Larcombe, 2, 130). Rates were especially badly handled. He also notes the presence of a few brave vigilantes and watchdogs, McElhone in the mid 1870s for example. But the ever cautious Larcombe also observes, 'whether vested interests had exercised pressure it is difficult to say' (130). Corruption even then tried to cover its tracks. Barrett (1979), writing of Melbourne, prefers the term jobbery to corruption (30). He draws attention to the general role and activities of the business community (302), but goes on to mention property valuations (181-3), contracts, quality of work and goods (201), favouritism in deciding where works should be executed (1971, 42), and night soil collection (1971, 127). He also provides one of very few Australian instances of the sinecure, on Melbourne's water supply commission in the 1850s (1979, 214). Dunstan (1984) emphasises patronage – 'billets for friends, relatives and party hacks' (37) – and abuse of inside information (91). He also notes that at some periods citizens of ability and experience took a more favourable view, in the 1850s for example (50-4) and that councillors' devotion to local interests certainly got things done (36). However in the same decade awareness of the possibility of corruption featured in discussion of the Municipal Institutions Establishment Bill 1854 (Barrett, 1919, 132) and Barrett makes frequent reference in this period to councillors' taking advantage of their position (1979, 181-3, 200; 1971, 42, 48-9, 58-61). At least one critic has emphasised the risk of exaggeration, regarding the corrupt aldermen who feature in many accounts as 'in general fiction' (Mayne, 1982, 223). Maybe so but the evidence, if not always the interpretation, of municipal corruption in the big cities is overwhelming. And it made a durable difference not only in establishing a tradition but in such terms as location of facilities, costs, and quality of life. The problem was never solved, commissions of enquiry, prosecutions, suspensions, and changes to legislation notwithstanding. The latter indicate the problems exacerbated by deficiencies of legislation. Thus 1895 legislation in New South Wales protected aldermen with interests in water, gas, electricity, paving, kerbing and guttering contracts (Maiden, 1966, 87).

The overall impression is of endemic corruption brought about by a combination of venal representatives and compliant officials in a climate of low commercial morality. The beneficiaries were the rich and well connected. Sydney's 'Great Water Meter Scandal of 1883' involved resetting meters for the favoured few, among them the mayor (Fitzgerald, 187, 77-8). Fitzgerald (81) ascribes the deservedly bad repute of the City Council's handling of water and sewage, eventually resulting in its loss of control, to 'inadequate funding and faulty legislation ... conducive to corrupt practices'. Her methodological position already noted deserves further comment, and can be summed up in the phrase 'So What!' (154). This phrase she takes from a common response to charges of corruption, and employs it in recognition of the reality of comment that this kind of charge can be levelled very widely, and in an attempt, well intentioned but arguably dangerous, to focus attention on endemic corruption rather than incidents. Her account of Sydney reads very much as the former, approaching the topic from the position that business people with council connexions enjoy advantages and that much corruption on the political left is defensible as a response to this situation (157-61). Whether or not one accepts that position she is exceptional among historians in the attention given both to the topic *per se* and to its definitional dimensions. The victims were the urban poor but given opportunity and occasion their representatives cut an equally dismal figure. If Labour representation began in glorious good faith and intention its degeneration was rapid and complete, but this is once more to anticipate.

It is of course tempting to assume that what prevailed in the big cities was more widely the case, a dangerous assumption awaiting exploration in areas where the concept of corruption itself needs adjustment. It is of interest to note however that Bate observes that Ballarat was initially corrupt but goes on to argue that this was soon overcome by attitudes of idealism and cooperation (1978, 24, 258). Was this a function of mining or of size? And note that Blainey (1969, 193) makes not dissimilar claims for West Australian gold towns towards the end of the century.

As to conceptual adjustment corruption in the cities evidently parallels that in state government – contracts, favouritism, patronage for example. However at the local scale the idea of conflict of interests becomes more and more difficult to apply. So often, though by no means invariably, community interest and a range of private interests converge to the point of correspondence. The alternative to ongoing public involvement of the business leaders – often also the sole practitioners and possessors of particular skills in a community – in its affairs becomes ridiculous. After all a scarcity of able men is one of the problems of municipal government in colonial Australia cited by its leading investigators.

Patronage

The persistence of patronage as the main avenue of recruitment, and to a lesser degree of advancement, within the public service of the six colonies would not have been assumed in mid-century. That it prevailed in the face of exercises in reform and the successful British example says something of the socio-economic state of the colonies – too little education, too many other opportunities, for recruitment on merit and by competition to succeed – and something of the attitude of parliamentarians and, more unexpectedly, of senior civil servants in whose control about half of all patronage resided (Knight, 1961, 177), patronage employed however in terms of favouritism rather than cash. The overall result was administrative weakness – low levels of competence let alone enterprise – and insecurity, both recipes for corruption. The exact situation seems to have varied from state to state: in the 1890s four-fifths of the staff in New South Wales were temporaries (Knight 1961, 174-6). This was the commonest form of using patronage. It is interesting in passing to note the problem of the temporary public servant was recognised in this context as early as the 1830s (Fletcher, 1979 (2), 274). The same problem is also a central feature of Wurth's study of the New South Wales public service since the 1895 reforms (Wurth, 1960, passim). Retrenchment also provided opportunities, as *The Bulletin* described it in 1894 (Knight, 1972, 252): 'the art and mystery of discharging a large, sensational body of able-bodied officials ... and then appointing quietly, one by one, a crowd of personal friends and supporters in their stead'. In the adjacent Victoria the abuse of patronage is a frequent topic in Turner's 1904 history, noting the presence in several government departments of 'all sorts of unfit hangers on' (2-242). An area that attracted most particular comment was the railways (Serle, 1971, 34). Note that in this case as with public works there are plenty of opportunities for the unskilled, a wide geographical spread of jobs, and a high risk of conspicuously unfortunate outcomes over and above any questions of cost.

Some Exceptions

Finally three areas where evidence and discussion is less than might be expected deserve brief mention. Electoral corruption was widespread. This was usually in the form of personation, not always illegal! (Nairn, 1967, 8), not peculiarly Australian, and declining. According to Trollope (1967, 259) intimidation and bribery were rare, except in Queensland. The parallels with Britain, save perhaps in method, are evident. More surprisingly the mining industry and communities – a major prop of Australia's meteorically rising living standard – do not emerge as evidently corrupt. The mining towns appear to have been rough, tough and honestly administered though Blainey as noted specifically reserves his adulation to Western Australia in the 1890s. The nature of the industry itself – in essence a form of gambling and the corrupter is not a gambler – and its infrastructures, where cooperation had to operate alongside individual enterprise, both acted against political corruption. That is not to deny the element of dishonesty and deception in the mining industry, of rorts and scams, but these worked less politically than commercially, especially against greedy or ill informed outside investors. Corruption in a loose sense, but not political corruption.

Nor does vice receive much contemporary discussion, especially by comparison with its present status as one of the core areas of Australian political corruption. Of course it existed, of course it had political connotations, but it was not yet up for public discussion, at least not very often. All our instincts and experience suggest that in a society concerned to regulate even supress the liquor trade, to clamp down on the sex trades, and beginning to have similar views about gambling, the police and politicians would be corrupted. The evidence is limited but it is impossible to believe that this is because vice and related corruption did not exist. It can more credibly be argued that what existed – probably a lot – sat more marginally to the political system than was soon to be the case, especially once operators such as John Wren got to work, in his case in Melbourne in the last decades of the nineteenth century. Our forebears in nineteenth century Australia did not merely disapprove – they did not much discuss.

Conclusion

To venture an interpretation of the role and place of political corruption in colonial Australia is to enter on a more complex task than is the case for the preceding period. Corruption had been central, intrinsic and inevitable in the preceding political order dominated by penal considerations, and that dominance possessed a momentum. Nevertheless a less corrupt or a differently corrupt colonial experience from what momentum and circumstance provided is by no means inconceivable. Land and infrastructure might have been managed rationally and honestly, cities governed equitably and fairly. That they were not is a fact of Australia's history and geography. Corruption made the difference of particular outcomes – of this not that – and in the remarkable context of the progress in one century from a half starved convict settlement to one of the wealthiest and most stable economies and societies in the world. Certainly this assessment requires qualification in such terms as environmental impact and sustainability, overall equity and the maltreatment of the indigenes, but it remains the fact that to be born a white Australian in the last quarter of the nineteenth century was to be born among the favoured few. Why else would Australia have been such a migrant magnet? Corruption was a matter of difference not, as it was and was to become in Latin America, of disaster. This is not to peripheralise corruption in looking at Australia but rather to argue that a sense of proportion in discussing a neglected issue is the appropriate counter to the temptations of reductionism. The other counter is the assessments made by contemporaries of the phenomenon. While many Australians of the colonial period were participants in the less honest elements of the political and administrative process, so too there were many, and also many visitors, willing to write about the state of colonial affairs. What is provided is not consensus but a range of insights. Thus Twopenny (1883, 191) noted that the high Victorian tariff engendered extensive (and skilful) false invoicing even among reputable firms, a practice politically corrupt to the extent that it depended upon the cooperation of public servants. On one view no one was deceived: not merely every visitor but everyone with eyes to see was aware of the existence of favouritism, nepotism, corruption, jobbing and occasionally direct bribery, that Australia was not run by the book, and that this was especially the case in the areas of land and public works. Development of this kind in the nineteenth century was rarely squeaky clean, and in Australia haste, centralisation, and popular expectations of how men in power would behave exacerbated the situation. One commentator argues that this is the context in which 'the characteristic political form of the countryside is not the local committee of management but the deputation' (Davies in Encel, 1970, 158-9), a context favourable to corruption. Trollope (1967, 682) commented that in new settled countries government was of necessity active and interfering, and that that situation carried with it the risk of its improper use for political purposes.

Fundamental to this situation on the view of some of the most experienced and discerning commentators was the fact that most Australians had come to the continent to make money, that this was the ethos of colonial Australia, and that in the absence or at least weakness of a range of constraints commonplace and familiar in Britain a degree of political corruption was to be expected and accepted. It was the price of progress, manifest not only in rural development but in city business. In the colonial period this interpretation quickly displaced, without quite destroying, an element of harking back to the convict past. It explained without quite justifying and left room for improvement. When Dilke paid a second visit to Australia in the late eighties he commented that Victoria, South Australia and Tasmania had 'as little corruption as in the mother country (Dilke, 1890, 2, 229) and that New South Wales had improved (Dilke, 1890, 2, 229). He may have been exaggerating, and he was certainly aware of problems in the public works area in New South Wales and Queensland (I, 272) and of the phenomenon of the 'Roads and Bridges' member. Interestingly he ascribed the Victorian improvement at least in part to payment of members (I, 200-1). Colonial Australia generally accepted a *modus vivendi* of corruption at quite a high level and hoped that it might be a more a transient phenomenon than in fact turned out to be the case. Corruption was tacitly accepted as the likely development experience in circumstances where a small population had to accomplish a great deal but an experience to be watched closely in the hope of its early diminution. And at least Australians gained the reputation of not being easily taken in. This position was realist rather than cynical and things were getting better. No one really expected the end of the colonies the coming of Commonwealth to end corruption. If corruption was an issue at all in the long discussions, it was a very peripheral one; but in the absence of effective campaigns against corruption the succeeding century saw change rather than diminution in the status and significance of political corruption in Australia. Another opportunity had been fudged if not completely missed.

Note

1   T.S. Eliot, *Murder in the Cathedral*, where it is described as the 'ultimate treason'!

5 Corruption Concealed – A Complacent Commonwealth

The newly established Commonwealth formalised and unified Australia's political identity while maintaining a considerable role – and thus political apparatus and activity – for the new states (erstwhile colonies). The relative absence of political corruption from Commonwealth politics has long been acknowledged. The Commonwealth dealt and deals in matters less susceptible than those which are the major concerns of state politics. It was well served by its first generation of parliamentarians and public servants who from a background at least tainted with corruption but also in many cases recently reformed were determined to distance Commonwealth government from that part of its colonial heritage, both the long standing tradition and the spectacular events of the 1890s.

Political corruption remained endemic and widespread but only occasionally spectacular in Australia during the first three quarters of the twentieth century. There exists a substantial body of source material but neither that material nor the issue in general has received a great deal of attention. Thus when a body of scholarly writing on Australian politics emerges the matter, as has been noted, is scarcely mentioned. Davis's (1960) treatment of the states' governments says little on the topic. Certainly neither the terms of reference nor the substance of the Wilenski reports on the government of New South Wales, prepared between 1977-82, nor Alaba's book on the reports give a strong position to political corruption (Alaba, 1994, 180). Mayer and Nelson's *Australian Politics: a third reader* (1973) claims that a chapter which touches on the topic is a first, but corruption gets no index mention and the bibliography musters two items on the subject. The remarkable claim is also made that the subject, at least in terms of councils and planning, is 'too big to treat here' (158). Most recently the third edition of Hughes' *Australian Politics* (1998) says nothing on local government and its meagre discussion of corruption (324-5) (no index entry) is subsumed into accountability with an inevitable loss of focus. Nevertheless valuable points are made, for example the significance of the extensive and substantially unconstrained character of state government. These in a sense encapsulate the standing of political corruption in this period, known to exist, ignored and understudied, but probably a bigger issue than anyone is ready or equipped to open up and pursue.

How is this situation to be accounted for and remedied? The context of this complacency provides a degree of explanation: the distraction of two world wars; continuing economic and social growth – by world standards Australia remained a lucky country – suggesting that nothing was too seriously amiss; a real improvement by comparison with the last decade of the nineteenth century. Carroll, writing at the end of the period, suggests that consumerism had led to lethargy, that Australians were less likely (than Americans) to become indignant about injustice or inefficiency'. But why the difference? (Carroll, 1978, 14-5). The relocation of the core of corruption into two areas harder to penetrate than their nineteenth century precursors – the smoke filled rooms of political parties and the corridors of power of state and local government – may also be significant. In this latter case quite a lot was unearthed, but the resultant verdict was episodic rather than endemic. At each level, state and municipal, though with exceptions in the latter, the process of government and politics had become well established. Recruitment had become if not solely a matter of merit more substantially so even if the best tended to drift to Canberra. Promotion was primarily a matter of seniority. As Australia settled down, a career in the state public service, or in local government became an increasingly attractive proposition. Its reputation was not quite unsullied: one senior officer of the New South Wales Public Service Board in 1978 described his role as to 'shop' (i.e. convict) corrupt heads of department, men who would have risen through the public service over perhaps forty years without being caught (Clark 1997, 161). Temporary appointments remained an evident part of the problem (Wurth, 1960, passim). The very nature of government activity at these levels required a burgeoning army of officials and clerks to carry out the decisions – commonly expenditure or regulatory decisions – of their masters, and often as Hallows (1970, 134-5) noted as a support service for private enterprise. The course was set towards state and local government as the great distributor of things and services, 'all those functions which seem to affect most his (the citizen's) economic and social wellbeing' (Hancock, 1930, 76). rarely concerned with ideas. This was to climax in the almost wholly executive and administrative apparatus characteristic of state government in the last decades of the century (Jaensch in Mayer and Nelson, 1980, 183).

What had not changed was habits of mind. As early as 1908 a writer from *The Times*, as reported by Encel in 1970 (58-9), notes an Australian habit of regarding the state as holding keys of success and failure, as something outside themselves, and which 'each interest must capture or conciliate for its own purposes lest others should capture it for theirs'. Later in the same work (58-9) A.F. Davies notes the Australian habit of 'leaning on the bureaucracy' and that the characteristic political form of the countryside is not the local committee of management but the deputation. A resentful dependency would summarise these evaluations.

The strands of corruption, and the issues of context and status have been discussed, but it remains curiously difficult to capture or recount corruption's essence in the first three quarters of twentieth century Australia by comparison with earlier periods. The first impression is of a few spectacular incidents – rogue waves – on a groundswell of endemic corruption insufficient to nauseate or even be noticed by most Australians, an impression only conceivably to be overturned by an exceptionally close and intense reading of sources possible only at a very local level. Most of what has been written is about the rogue; and such extreme cases are not good indicators of the real world especially when their connexion to the more mundane is so uncertain. The not infrequent instances of enquiries with negative or non-committal findings of which Davis enumerated eight in New South Wales between 1900 and 1960 (Davis, 1960, 128-30) naturally receive relatively little attention by comparison. At this point this book runs too far ahead of the body of detailed scholarship and sources for comfort and is even more emphatically a call for further work than earlier and later chapters.

Our subject matter represents for the most part a continuation of the colonial phenomenon, but both its content and context have changed. Two traditionally significant areas – land alienation and railway building – had almost run their course. Others remained, patronage, public works and general municipal administration. A third category represents evolution and emergence: land-use becomes an important urban issue, suburban streets and subdivisions. One writer rather dismissively described the states as 'a sort of super town-planning authority' (Hallows, 1970, 120), and also noted that it was rather left to the old guard.

Patronage

Late nineteenth century and early twentieth century reform often focused on patronage. It was one step forward, at times a bold one, but rarely a durable one. Old habits died hard and/or creep back. Within five years of the establishment of the Public Service Board of New South Wales corruption featured, albeit not centrally, in a critical estimate (Wurth, 1960,

291). Not all criticism is however to be taken seriously: was the appointment of the father of a Board Member's wife's second cousin's wife really nepotism? (296). As to the consequences of patronage Fitzgerald (1992, 166), a thoughtful commentator but with a tendency to condone as often as to criticise, remarks as to its effects on standards of work in the period after 1945.

Land

As far as land is concerned there is run of the mill evidence for continuance of old practices, dummying in Tasmania as late as 1910 (Tasmania, 1910 (1), ix. Roberts (1924, 362) notes that in the period 1890-1920, in New South Wales, when there was considerable repurchase for closer settlement the administrative process was either corrupt or negligent or both. The most famous and most fully reported instance culminated in the already discussed Royal Commission presided over by Justice Owen in 1906 (Pearl, 1958; NSW, 1906 (1) and (2)). (Interestingly Owen's son was a leading anti-corruption campaigner in the 1930s.) The matters in question, ministerial receipt of bribes for improvement leases via numerous agents, payments of tens of thousands of pounds relating to almost ten thousand square miles, were far from trivial. The interest of the enquiry however lies as much in the procedural problems encountered by Owen, a result of inadequate legislation, a half-hearted legislature, and perhaps the climate of public opinion, in the face of several very determined and resourceful accused who were eventually exposed but never successfully brought to trial. The enquiry itself exposed not merely the expected: confusion and wilful self deception as to conflict of interest (present in eight of twelve cases); the role of a compliant departmental official 'too eager to carry out the wishes of the Minister, irrespective of the reports of the officers' (NSW, 1906 (1), 74); the centrality of cash payments. There was also a great deal that was less expected: the return of unsuccessful bribes; the existence of written accounts (perhaps because of the size of the operation – and were they true and accurate records?). Two important discoveries from the scholarly perspective are: the confirmation of the importance of the land agent MP, almost essential for a favourable and expeditious outcome and expecting to be well paid; and the centrality of a very high degree of ministerial and administrative discretion arguably beyond what was necessary or intrinsic to the matter in hand. Nor did the issue ever quite disappear, for example ministerial bribes in 1956 (Queensland, 1956). In 1958-9 (Lack, 1962, 717-20) parliamentarian's conflicts of interest in

Queensland with respect to Crown leases were the subjects of official enquiry. More generally Troy (1978) notes a number of state level enquiries in the years around 1970.

Railways and Public Works

By comparison with such incidents and enquiries there is little to be said about the railways and tramways. Construction was largely complete although Bent was found to have misled the Victorian parliament in one case (among six) to his own financial advantage in 1909 (Victoria, 1909). Bate, the historian of Bent's home base of Brighton, perspicaciously notes (249): 'he had so many interests in the town that whatever was done was gain to him'. Other enquiries cleared Bent, but other writers would view him less favourably (Davidson, 1970, 177-9). A vast Tasmanian Royal Commission in 1910 (Tasmania, 1910 (2)) took 16000 questions to clear the Chief Engineer, Lieutenant Governor and Minister of Lands and Works of allegations of corruption. A mature and essential railway system gave more opportunity on the operational side, as a West Australian enquiry in 1901 (West Australia, 1901) concerning railway officials and the Perth Ice Company – peculiarly vulnerable by the nature of its business – discovered. The extent of such activity is impossible even to guess at. The Perth case was certainly not at the petty margin but does no more than indicate the seizure of an ubiquitous opportunity. The New South Wales Legislative Council report on the Public Works Department in 1911 suggests the presence of a few dishonest officials rather than a structural problem. In some matters and areas *ad hoc* authorities proved the answer to such traditional problems as nepotism and interference with the tendering process, in Queensland in the inter-war years for example (Laverty, 1972, 277).

Planning

As the traditional version of corruption in the land resource area diminishes another takes its place, land-use planning particularly in urban areas. It is today both a central and familiar dimension of local government, one with which the citizen is likely to come into direct contact, and one with a global taint of corrupt practice. As in most developed countries its effective establishment in a modern version in Australia dates from the years after 1945 (Burnley, 1974, 203-6) by the states but in response to

Commonwealth legislation. Its basis was not only of new hopes but old fears based on the unhappy experience of inadequate regulation in the inter-war years. Before that it was a matter of experiment, and not a little eccentricity, except where basic services were concerned. However the Australian experience of land-use planning must be looked at in a context of the experience of organised settlement over a long time period, not only in building cities but also more generally in occupying land and developing resources. The backward linkages of modern planning, now an established profession in its own right for half a century, are with both local and state government, with the states' lands departments, with the surveying profession and with municipal engineering, the first home and parent of many city planning departments.

It is then neither difficult nor surprising to find examples of corruption in the planning process, especially after World War Two as the rules became stricter and the pressures greater. And it should also be noted, as Tiffen observes (1999, 129) that real estate deals almost unavoidably leave a paper trail. It is of planning that Mayer and Nelson (1973, 158) make their 'too big to tackle' comment, citing in support an enquiry into Brisbane City in 1967. Interestingly the chapter is headed 'Disobedience and Democracy'. However Hollander's 1997 account of the Queensland Housing Commission in the immediate post-war period suggests no more than a modest level of corruption. In general, however, the ubiquitousness and familiarity of the phenomenon almost make comment superfluous. Planners, inspectors, councillors, officials, developers all played a predictable part – and made a difference.

Thus Sandercock's investigations of Melbourne in the 1970s (1975, 1979) suggest a widespread phenomenon with emphasis upon inside information in such instances as the Melbourne Underground, Westernport, and the Victoria Housing Commission. Investigations in the early 1970s were inconclusive (1979, 20-22) but raised the perennial issue of the propriety or otherwise of councillor and council official involvement in land dealings. Allegations relating to the Chairman of the Melbourne Board of Works, that he made almost half a million dollars corruptly from land sales in the period 1961-72, also failed (Tiffen, 1999, 64). A 1978 Board of Enquiry (Victoria, 1978) found that corruption in the commission was broad based, involving officials (one officer received a relatively modest $31556 between 1973 and 1975), estate agents and finance companies; prosecutions were barred by lapse of time. The worst experience was in Sydney: in fifteen years between 1952 and 1967 three councils were dissolved because they had been proved to be thoroughly corrupt in this respect (Kriak-Krai, chapter 4). Total dismissal however did not mean that every councillor (let alone every council) was corrupt. It was simply an unsatisfactory dimension – a legal problem in getting rid of individual councillors – of a more widely weak and unsatisfactory legal framework for the pursuit of corruption. It was moreover a pursuit not highly favoured by state governments – political parties were beginning to be beneficiaries – notably in New South Wales where in 1952 gagging legislation sought to inhibit media exposure (Kriak-Krai, 66-74). It was not durably effective, but the public opinion which overturned it was scarcely clamorous in its concern to see corruption exposed, and there was later some tendency even among newspapermen to cast a favourable gloss over at least the 1950s (Terrill, 1987, 281). In other words the initial period of in principle rigorous urban land-use planning coincided with a period of relative complacency, even hostility, as far as exposure of corruption was concerned. By the 1970s allegations of planning corruption in Sydney were again common (Daly, 1982, 115 and 26) and the close links between premier Askin and particular property and financial interests were well known (Head, 1986, 103-4). It is almost surprising that more was not exposed and interesting to note that although mentioned corruption does not feature prominently in either Head's or Daly's work. We may never know how much actually occurred and the true extent of its geography.

Vice

The connection between vice – drink, gambling and sex – and political corruption is one that has been made public rather than transformed. It is a connection scarcely to be doubted during the nineteenth century, but peripheralised by the more obvious political and public significance of other facets of corruption – land and the commissariat for example – and by a degree of reticence, even prudery, on matters of sex. Morality certainly provided the starting point for political concern as to vice: it is not however the best way into the topic in terms of its propensity to generate corruption. That comes at the end point, the decision at least to regulate and sometimes to bar, and its enforcement by the police.

A succession of official enquiries into police forces manifest the long standing prevalence of corruption and its particular forms, often in great detail. Swanton's (1985) paper on James Mitchell (Inspector General and then Commissioner of New South Wales police 1915-30) encapsulates this situation in remarking that his career was 'significant for its lack of personal scandal and adverse comment' (284). Three quarters of the causative factors identified in a 1992 account of police corruption (Moir and Eijkman, 1992, 108-9) were long standing. It has also been widespread. Thus a 1958 report reckoned that 60% of enforcing officers in the Victorian gaming squad were corrupt and that the position was worse in New South Wales (but the witness was from Victoria!) (Finnane, 1994, 174-5). In New South Wales at this period testimonial evenings for members of the force retiring from the licensing squad were regularly attended by bookmakers and hoteliers (Finnane, 1994, 175). In the 1970s one New South Wales police superintendent allegedly received $A1000 per month from a 'prominent racing identity with connections to organised crime' (Steketee and Cockburn, 1986, 275) Even in South Australia a generation earlier the 1927 Royal Commission found 10 of 22 officers charged corrupt. In this case the accused officers' financial position was the strongest evidence. Not only the police were involved: a Tasmanian Premier in the 1930s was more than suspect in the area of licensing and bookmaking, a Treasurer in 1950 in lottery licensing (Robson, 1991, 2, 432-3, 537). Bookmakers were allegedly financing on a modest scale – the sum of $3000 is mentioned – the Tasmanian Labour Party in the 1970s (Townley, 318-23). Political protection for illegal casinos in Victoria in the 1970s cost the state a spectacular $1.4 million in revenue per annum and a substantial part of the proceeds went to the state premier, $A2000 per week from one casino alone (Steketee and Cockburn, 1986, 263-4). In general terms corruption features frequently in O'Hara's (1988) history of gambling in Australia, mostly in connection with horse racing and a great deal of it political, at levels ranging from the beat constable to the state premier. Illegal SP bookmaking[1] features conspicuously in his discussion (226-41).

It would nevertheless be a mistake to regard police corruption as universal. The South Australian enquiry referred to above also reported the closure of a number of gaming houses and that since 1920 arrests and removals had numbered never less than 600 and in some years more than 1000 annually. Two interesting but very different case studies are Hasluck's assertion (Hasluck, 1977, 101-7) that the brothels of Perth in the 1920s were regulated by the police – a 'tolerated houses' system – without corruption, an assertion based on his experience as a newspaperman; and Frank Hardy's Marxist account (1963) of rural police corruption in the 1930s, an account with functionalist sympathies somewhat surprising given his hard line position in *Power Without Glory*. Evidence of investigative incompetence should occasion no surprise given that police corruption was evidently no more than the visible centre of a wider web. Thus enquiries into illegal SP betting in West Australia in 1948 and 1959 did not even look at the police (Finnane, 1994, 175). Investigation was always difficult, confronted by a police code of silence, the risk of depending on the evidence of less than reputable witnesses (Victoria, 1933, passim), and by substantially hostile public opinion seeking freedom to gamble, drink and whore as they pleased. The inevitable political response, denial of the problem or resort to the 'bad apple' remains as it was then unconvincing. It is out of tune with the evidence for widespread and organised police corruption 'more often than isolated or occasional' at the very least to quote a 1965 comment (Victoria, 1978 (2), 61). Finally both the peculiarly pernicious status of police corruption, and Finnane's observation (1994, 176) that police corruption is often well organised to the point of playing 'an active role in their modes of organisation' deserve reiteration. This is to reiterate and reinterpret Horne's 1985 comment ('Australia: Terra Incognita', 185) that 'where one of the actual, if unintended, functions of the police is corruption ..., its style becomes one of continuing hypocrisy and cover up'.

One book encapsulates, at a local level, the experience of vice driven police corruption in Australia through the first half of the twentieth century, Frank Hardy's *Power Without Glory*. Its central figure, John Wren, is a thinly disguised version of John West, a Labour Party supporter, who built an empire and a reputation primarily on illegal gambling and associated police corruption in Melbourne but also on personal generosity. Hardy, a hard line Marxist, and no angel, was a certainly courageous figure whose book generated a famous trial for criminal libel in which he was memorably acquitted. The rapt and enthusiastic reception of a television version of the novel in the 1970s testifies to its accuracy, although West was defended and continues to be defended from a variety of perspectives in some Labour Party quarters. Less well known but equally cogent and relevant is Hardy's fictional account of a srike in the refuse and night soil section of a suburban Sydney municipality in the 1960s, based on an actual incident. *The Outcasts of Foolgarah* (1971) is, predictably, a bawdy Marxist account with frequent unambiguous references to well known political figures. Mentions of corruption abound, focusing upon garbage contracts, land development, inside information (priced at a retainer of $8000 a year), and conflict of interest. They carry conviction despite the otherwise bizarre character of the work.

Governance in General

Two traditional components of political corruption commonplace in twentieth century Australia – planning and policing – are well defined. For a third – the general business of governance – this is much less the case and discussion is complicated by a changing and controversial connexion with the party system which is of such importance as to require separate discussion. One important part of general administration – state and municipal – is the continuation, corruption included, of a diversity of activities as old as European settlement, public works and contracts in general. In terms of corruption these are the subject of frequent reference during this period, cartage, coal and roads in Sydney in the 1920s for example, a period of notorious corruption, of 'a complete contempt for citizen welfare' in the words of Larcombe the historian of local government (3, 46). *The Sydney Morning Herald* compared the political machine of that period with Tammany (Larcombe, 3, 42). Larcombe also commented on the greater politicisation of the corruption of the 1920s by comparison with the 1850s (46). In 1927 the city council was sacked on these grounds not for the first time (Kriak-Krai, 56-8). But Sydney is just the most explored instance, probably the most corrupt but certainly not the only such. In Tasmania in the 1940s bus routes were the domain of corruption (Robson, 2, 531). Elsewhere instances of general corruption probably comparable to Sydney occurred. At Williamstown (Victoria) in 1930 a Royal Commission found misappropriation of roading funds for private use, improper tendering, electoral fraud, improper dismissals, fictitious pay rolls, and misuse of information. No report was printed, somewhat surprisingly (though archival material is available), suggestive perhaps of political pressure to minimise publicity. Radbone (1981, 78) similarly comments that the South Australian government was keen to investigate but reluctant to publish with respect to misconduct in the Licensing Court in the 1920s. Kriak-Krai (1971, 195) writing of New South Wales at some length notes the weakness of the state's Local Government Department in its role as regulator of municipalities, and notes the general problem of a legal system which made it hard to bring charges of corruption (11). But his broader evaluation is of a political environment not favourable to corruption. Given that he finds a great deal of it to discuss, and detailed factual discussion is the main strength of the work, the assessment is rather unconvincing. Not only scholars such as Kriak-Krai, writing at the end of the period, could be so deceived. MacKenzie (1962, 30), an overseas visitor and in many respects a shrewd and perceptive commentator, regarded New South Wales as a well-run and efficiently administered state. Probably the most spectacular example of local level corruption was at Bankstown in 1954 when control was seized by a corrupt group willing to go as far as to bomb the local newspaper office (Kriak-Krai, 1971, 89). He goes on to note that when an administrator replaced the council the area improved remarkably.

As already mentioned neither the law nor the political establishment made it easy to investigate or take action. Thus the Royal Commission into Bunnerong allegedly allowed some to escape (Fitzgerald, 1992, 236). Kennedy writing of Queensland in the early 1920s (1979, 66), almost a decade prior to the Mungana affair which was the subject of his later book, while regarding bribery as rare yet noted that it was widely suspected at a local level because public office holders and the business community had such close – I would add inevitable – connexions and that they were rarely exposed. From a late twentieth century perspective the 1920s appear a particularly bad period, favoured by a context of social turmoil, and the period 1930-50 – depression and war – relatively clean. In general terms – and Sydney and Williamstown were extremes – the verdict must be widespread, intermittent, and normally rather low level. Kriak-Krai (1971, 15-16) notes that on average one municipal council member a year was convicted of 'corruption' in the late 1960s.

Much less is known or at least written about corruption in country areas during this period. Wild's work (1974) suggests some modest corruption in the process of supplying goods and services at the local level, and hints at the existence of other issues which cannot be included for legal reasons. He does not discuss planning. Gray (1991) is likewise generally silent but reports one councillor articulating the case that centralisation of regulation generates corruption (99).

Several particular incidents deserve note because of the exte.it to which they anticipate the changed circumstances of later decades. The Mungana affair – the sale of worthless mines to the state government of Queensland by cabinet ministers – has been thoroughly explored by Kennedy (1978). Its wider significance – at federal level – was at least in part a matter of chance. More important is the scale of the swindle and the way in which it brings state ministers and big business into close and questionable contact, two characteristics of recent decades, but then more exceptional. The scandal as to Sydney's Bunnerong power plant at roughly the same date has similar attributes, linking city council and international big business (Fitzgerald, 1992, 236). Comalco offered cheap shares to Queensland ministers in the 1970s (Fitzgerald, 1984, 311-3). British tobacco interests attempted to bribe Tasmania's Lands Minister over a development scheme in the 1970s (Townley, 1973, 323). International dimensions became significant in the corruption scandals of the last decade of the century. The sums involved in the Bunnerong case were certainly large (whether viewed as extortion or bribe or both), £10000 to £15000 compared to the much lower indeed exceptionally low levels of ordinary municipal contracts at the same period £50 on a £10000 (i.e. 1/2%) cartage contract for example (Kriak-Krai, 1971, 51-6).

Political Parties

Bunnerong also serves to introduce the final major issue for consideration in this chapter both in its own right and in anticipation of subsequent events. In his memoirs written a generation later Lang (1956, 374), one time Labour premier of New South Wales, commented: 'there must be two parties to any illicit transaction ... Who is the more guilty?' This was at the time a more cogent and perceptive view than it appears now when this perspective can almost be taken for granted. Discussion of Bunnerong at the time was highly politicised and the allegations and accusations were in some quarters defended along the familiar lines that Labour was simply seizing opportunities which were available to it only within the political situation. Its opponents, in many cases businessmen, allegedly possessed, by contrast, a wider range of opportunities arising not only from their political activities but more generally, in hiring workers for example. This may or may not be a valid argument, but it is one which was certainly advanced at the time and since and which requires discussion. More generally the period 1900-1975 witnesses the entrenchment of political parties into state and local government in an increasingly organised (and thus expensive) form. Again here are to be found the antecedents of a form of political corruption conspicuous and controversial in the last decades of the twentieth century, and not merely in Australia, that related to political parties and their financial needs.

Political corruption presupposes politics but not political parties. It was alive and well in nineteenth century Australia both before and while political parties came into being and as late as 1900 was a phenomenon not usually explored or discussed in party terms even though something like the modern party system had been created. The situation now is almost the reverse: political parties play a key role – even an exaggerated role – in discussion of political corruption. One commentator regards their role together with that of urban local government as the heartland of Australian political corruption, displacing state government *per se* (Parker, 1978, 9). The first three-quarters of the twentieth century establish this transformation. But what is the nature of the party component of political corruption and how does it relate to our definition of corruption?

Political parties may be corrupt, *sensu strictu*, in two ways. They may reward their members or supporters with jobs, contracts, decisions in circumstances where the rules say this is inappropriate, that merit, cost or rationality should decide. The antecedents of this situation in the 'old corruption' are self-evident and nineteenth century reformers – targeting that phenomenon – emphasised the need to depoliticise all sorts of areas of government activity. In Australia they were only partially successful: politicians and senior public servants resisted attacks on patronage and colonial and state governments retained a high degree of decision taking power at the centre with a high discretionary and political input. This was a kind of political corruption and became party political corruption when it ceased to be a matter of the individual minister, member or civil servant deciding and passed into the hands of the party or machine, locally or centrally. Even so its status was debatable: 'the allocation of barrow licences like the allocation of market stalls and hotels and shops in council resumption areas was widely understood to be a fertile area for rorting, variously understood as corrupt practice or as just reward for valued kin and party faithful' (Fitzgerald, 1992, 247). Note that the spectrum here extends from petty to sizeable corruption and that its Australian history goes back to the penal period. It was always more a problem for the Labour Party than for those on the right, though as Fitzgerald (1992, 236) points out the Sydney experience does not suggest that rich men are not amenable to bribes. They had resources with which to reward their supporters outside as well as within the political system – contracts, jobs – and were as men of business better able to profit from inside information, a branch of corruption in any event taken less seriously a century ago. As the workers' party Labour had much less opportunity of this kind outside politics – rewards to the faithful (jobs for the boys) had to be found within the system. This argument in various forms has been used to defend Labour from the accusation that it was the party of corruption. It was not the only such party and the argument is more an explanation than a defence or justification.

By contrast the focus in the late decades of the twentieth century is rather upon the nexus between party finance and corruption. Political parties become expensive to run, especially at elections, and one way of raising funds on a scale now impossible to achieve by the traditional means, of mass personal or trade union support, is to extract large donations from key supporters – big business (again note the asymmetry between right and left) – in return for ... for what? There is nothing wrong in parties espousing and implementing policies which appeal to particular groups: it is intrinsic and inevitable. Again corruption arises at the particular level, when the generous donor rather than the most competitive tenderer gets the contract, when planning rules are bent, over-ruled or ignored in favour of particular developers, when particular narrow interests are favoured over broader political intentions (often as expressed in a manifesto). This is to anticipate succeeding chapters as well as to cast a glance backward towards earlier discussions.

The establishment of political parties in at least proto-modern form in late nineteenth century Australia was quickly followed by party political corruption along the lines indicated in the first of the two definitional discussions above, a corruption more to do with modifying the management, in a discriminatory fashion, of the distribution of largesse than with raising funds, more apparent (but probably no more real) in the case of Labour than its opponents. The classic account, MacCalman's *Struggletown* (1984) (i.e. Richmond, an inner suburb of Melbourne), pulls no punches. Labour won control of the council in 1913: 'within a decade … (it) had acquired the evil reputation for corruption … that has dogged it ever since' (35). The classic forms were manifest: nepotism, petty corruption, favouritism, electoral fraud, planning. If the scale was extensive the financial dimension was probably modest at least until the 1960s when activity peaked, to be brought to a halt by official enquiry in 1982. The book is a crushing rebuff to the argument that corruption is a victimless crime, an argument not far removed from that which sees it as Labour's natural and only response to a structural disadvantage. Thus the 1982 enquiry found that the elderly for example were poorly and expensively provided for by corrupt contractors. This contrasts strongly with Cairns' defence (McCalman, 274) of the Labour machine: in summary 'not a bad sort of corruption I suppose'. His position, echoed by some others, reiterated that the Labour Party machine corruption was a lesser evil than the commercial advantage taken by many councillors in better off municipalities' and that 'jobs' were fuel and lubricant for the machine.

As party politics extended its grip and domain so political corruption became more and more party political corruption, something expected of parties by citizens and increasingly central to the operations of political parties. Over a period of about three-quarters of a century a party centred version of political corruption came to displace rather than to destroy its precursors. In Terrill's words both major parties discovered 'the therapeutic value of … rewarding your friends … punishing your enemies' (1987, 106). The situation came almost to be taken for granted and as already noted was not lacking in powerful apologists. This may even suggest an interpretation of Hancock's remarkable observation (1930, 211) that Labour 'had done a great deal to free political life from the political anarchy of local jobbing'. An extra and powerful player at a different scale had joined the game and the game began to develop rules. It remained a destructive sort of game. There are of course dangers of exaggeration, as well as the huge areas (especially rural) of which we know next to nothing. Both Larcombe, the leading historian of New South Wales local government and Krik-Krai tend to downplay the party dimension. What should not be downplayed, the most useful interpretation, is the role of party corruption in providing a platform on which the more extreme and individualistic manifestations of recent decades developed.

Conclusion

An overview of the place of political corruption in the first seventy-five years of Commonwealth Australia would then locate the phenomenon at state and local (especially city) level as the continuance of an established situation but would also recognise the changes that occurred – not necessarily an overall increase – in response to the external and internal context – population increase, economic change and regulation, public attitudes, and the role of parties in political activity. In detail political corruption presents an invariably unattractive picture of injustice and greed, but while this is the case for this period it does not amount in total to a picture of national shame and degradation, simply of comfortable and often ignorant complacency. By the 1970s this is changing – for both better and worse. Costigan and then Fitzgerald unveil activities and unleash forces of, by comparison, tidal dimensions. What they exposed was not only bigger and more spectacular than what had quietly gone on in preceding decades, at least as far as we can make even crude comparisons, but it roused public opinion and transformed established attitudes. The scene is set for a final substantive chapter looking at an Australia where corruption is conspicuously present though no longer taken for granted, is often the core of political and public debate, of which the true dimensions are more exactly known and the vital characteristics more completely understood, and where pre-eminently it ceases to be acceptable political behaviour.

Note

1 SP betting is betting with a bookmaker at the starting price, i.e. at the odds prevailing on the racecourse at the start of the race. Off-course (i.e. non racetrack) SP betting has long been and remains illegal in most of Australia. It is probably the most important though not the only kind of corruption associated with Australia's racing industry, but its incidence and importance has diminished since off-course betting (totalisator rather than SP) became legal from the 1960s.

6 Contemporary

It is now almost impossible to open an Australian metropolitan daily newspaper without finding at least one corruption story; often enough it is on the front page. The Australian media have during the last decade not so much discovered political corruption as recognised (and in the process reevaluated) its place in Australian politics and society. Scandal has come to be treated as substance, the epidemic regarded as the endemic. Not even the most alarmist media sources regard this as indicative of a massive increase in corruption. While there is some evidence of increase, or perhaps extension is a better word, the most rational position on this point remains an open agnosticism. What cannot be doubted is that public interest and concern has greatly increased and with it both the intellectual and practical responses of discussion and action. Corruption has come to occupy a central role in Australian politics – academic discourse perhaps excepted – even if usage remains loose and imprecise. The now almost proverbial distaste of Australians for politicians springs as much from a belief that they can be and have been corrupted as from any other cause. This is a healthy situation, far removed from both the traditional acceptance of the inevitability of corruption and the complacency, cover up, and confusion characteristic of many countries where corruption is a much bigger problem than in Australia. It is one which many Australian politicians and public servants have problems coming to terms with. If, however, this is a feature of the 1990s simultaneous with world wide changes in our understanding of political corruption, it is necessary to look back a further decade to discern the events which precipitated change.

Australia, the states in particular, has never been short on enquiry in this area. However, and as has been noted, two more recent official enquiries captured public attention and imagination to an exceptional extent, not least because the hostile response of many politicians tended to confirm the widespread opinion that something was seriously wrong. The enquiries in question, by Costigan in the early eighties and Fitzgerald in the mid-eighties – handy shorthand in lieu of their lengthy titles – concerned in the first case 'the activities of the Federated Ship Painters and Dockers Union' initially in Melbourne but eventually nationally, and in the second initially police corruption but eventually 'a fundamental investigation into

90

the way things have been done ... for a very long time' (Coaldrake and Wanna, 1989, 413) in Queensland.

Costigan set out to look at the Melbourne waterfront and allegations of union malpractice and violence. The molehill became a mountain range. The final huge report (1984) requires nine pages to list the lawyers briefed and lists well over a thousand exhibits. Size, scope and the emphasis on the political connexions of organised crime captured attention as much as particular incidents, and if corruption was not the core of the enquiry it cropped up at almost every point. Among the enquiry's many foci were: corporate fraud; the role of the banks; tax evasion; drugs; the corruptive role of illegal SP bookmaking *vis à vis* the police; the element of long term continuity in the persons involved; the essential role of secrecy. The report itself is in a sense unsatisfactory with many blank pages and several unpublished volumes on account of ongoing proceedings, but it carries conviction. What makes it a bench mark however is the political response. Initially supportive, Prime Minister Hawke rapidly shifted ground and wound up an incomplete enquiry. On one view his reason was that Costigan had got too close to important people for the politicians' comfort. Also rejected by the politicians were key ideas such as a National Crime Authority and tax crime investigation, and access was refused to documents allegedly linking corruption to the United States Central Intelligence Agency (Pilger, 1992, 317-8). Public interest may not have been universally outraged but it was aroused.

Fitzgerald's Queensland report while less extensive covered an enormous range of activities from a very specific starting point – the police. This extension necessitated several, and at times much criticised, alterations to the terms of reference. What he was after, and achieved, was to communicate a sense of systemic corruption in what was at the time one of the two most thoroughly corrupt Australian states. This he achieved to the extent that in 1989 corruption dominated the state election (Whip and Hughes, 1991). The most disturbing finding was that in a state where, as in most of Australia, cabinet took detailed decisions, any sense of conflict of interest appeared absent. Conflicts relating to shareholdings, land, mines and family businesses were just not considered (Bennett, 1992, 138-9). The broader political reaction suggests Queensland was not peculiar: 'ministers elsewhere were stunned at the fact that the (Queensland) ministers should have been charged for what has been normal behaviour for many' (Bennett, 1992, 138), and the general public by such details as the manifest links between corruption of this kind and organised crime. It is no surprise that public confidence in politicians rapidly evaporated: at worst the public would believe anything – but at best they would accept new measures.

They certainly had their interest aroused by initially particular investigations (Clark *et al.*, 1997, 110-11) indicating a general malaise. What was its pathology?

Any account of the pathology must explore symptoms and circumstances in general. Costigan and Fitzgerald are no more than a starting point for an enquiry which must connect with prior conditions. Political corruption in late twentieth century Australia had grown, inexorably and with few evident discontinuities out of the past. Its distinctiveness resided more in aggregate and scale than particularity or innovation.

The two states where it received most attention – not necessarily where it was on any scale most important for as Russell (Clark *et al.*, 1997, 163-4) points out maladministration to the point of crisis in state government was widespread in the 1980s – were Queensland and West Australia, peripheral to the Commonwealth's long standing centres of political and economic gravity, but simple and spectacular examples of government gone wrong. In these cases too there exists for the first time (and thus exceptionally) a sizeable body of secondary literature, journalism of various calibres and categories, devoted to exposure of corruption. The scholarly researcher can therefore rest his work on a firmer and more accessible base.

Queensland becomes famous, and on a global scale, for its political corruption in the 1980s under the right wing government of the flamboyant Johannes Bjelke-Petersen. What was going on has been well summarised by Coaldrake (1989) – donations from successful contractors, land sales to supporters without consultation or tender, favouritism in contested decisions, a blurring of any distinction between private and public interest, and between government and party. As the *Economist* (8 July 1989) put it: 'rigged electoral boundaries set the stage for the rigging of practically everything else'. This was not an innovation. As early as 1962 MacKenzie (220) had referred to its particular reputation in a book on Australia as a whole. Perhaps it would have been better if his sobriquet 'Bananaland' had caught on more widely. It is also interesting to note that Charlton, writing in 1983, provides a hostile account of the Bjelke-Petersen regime without much more than a hint of corruption save in a very general sense. With Coaldrake and Fitzgerald the cat is truly out of the bag. Queensland's political corruption was not historically peculiar to governments of the right. But apparently a massive increase in known corruption occurred from the 1970s in particularly favourable circumstances. These were right wing government with the protection of a large and gerrymandered majority and a traditional public lack of interest. The government – more accurately the party – could do what it liked and even passed legislation in 1981 legitimising secret deals not even scrutinised by cabinet (Fitzgerald, 1984, 395). Scrutiny by commissions and committees was equally discouraged (Weller, 1994, 16). The press was initially inactive (Tiffen, 1999, 238-9). Intolerance of dissent has also been noted as characteristic (Clarke, *et al.*, 1997, 7). Corruption was, in Coaldrake and Wanna's words (1989, 404) 'continuous, secure, orderly and protected'. Very large sums were involved. Thiess allegedly paid a million (Australian) dollars to the premier in the period 1981-4 to obtain, or on one view expedite (Charlton, 1982, 217-22), a contract. Among other areas of corruption in the 1980s were hospital and railway contracts, public works, diversion of dairy quotas to an area where they benefited party identities, sales of National Park land, and waterfront industry contracts. In Smith's words: 'the state (was) the instrument for securing private rewards' (Patience, 1985, 26). 'Hypocrisy (and) brazen greed' (Coaldrake and Wanna, 1989, 404) were to bring about its downfall, the starting point being, as noted, police corruption (Fitzgerald's original brief). Significantly this was an area where corruption may directly impinge on the man in the Brisbane omnibus. Nevertheless popular complacency took some undermining. Whip and Hughes found that corruption excited little electoral interest before 1986 (1991, 60-70) when Bjelke-Petersen retained office and strengthened his position. As Fitzgerald notes the ballot box is not a powerful check on executive power (Peachment, 1991, 139). Only in 1989 was the government defeated, and one consequence was a deal of exposure and establishment of a formal investigative body such as had hitherto been absent and indeed avoided. The point this body most vigorously makes is the prevalence of corruption in local government, in planning and on the Gold Coast (Queensland CJC, 1991). Such detailed investigation informs us as to not only the scale of the activity – $300000+ to the Mayor from tourism interests, as the Commission notes 'petty cash to a developer' (9). It also examines its ethos, a focus at macro scale – getting the correct party in power rather than particular decisions – and some of its methods, the designation of the payments as business expenses rather than payment to candidates. On one view this latter might be regarded as an exercise in legitimation or self deception: the tourist industry performing as an energetic and effective lobbyist. The size of the payment and its direction at a particular powerful individual discredits this line of argument. Queensland has now enjoyed a decade of argument and activity on the subject, a substantial but incomplete clean up, and levels of awareness for the moment render relapse unlikely. But political memories are short: it requires the delivery of evident benefits to securely establish political corruption as beyond the pale.

Interpretations of the corruption of Queensland politics in the 1970s and 1980s commonly emphasise its historical dimensions, the 'development for all, at any price, and without too much thought' philosophy characteristic of the state throughout its history (Fitzgerald, 1982, 114-5), the low status of education and of intellectual concerns in general by comparison with a get things done pragmatism, the marginalisation of the legislative and regulatory role of parliament in favour of a primacy for executive action. These are extreme instances even parodies of elements present in most of Australia's history and geography. What made things much worse in Queensland was the developing structure of political institutions in the hands of particular individuals, some of them essentially authoritarian and others simply very greedy, together with the surge of development during these decades in which Queensland attracted a much larger share of investment than in any earlier period. This investment had a large international dimension much of it connected with land development which frequently came into conflict with environmental concerns. It is then appropriate to see Queensland's corruption as reiteration of the colonial experience, but reiteration with differences of scale and scope, in essence the big international and multinational element. Public hostility engendered by its excesses, as belatedly exposed in the media, brought an end to the phenomenon, and laid it open for research, but does not alone guarantee against re-emergence.

The other *cause célèbre* of the 1980s and 1990s, West Australia, presents numerous parallels with Queensland. The state is and was a resource rich state traditionally as remote from Australian federal politics as its location suggests, which in the 1980s was vigorously pursuing development at any price policies in a favourable political environment. Of particular interest are accounts of West Australian politics immediately prior to the arousal of concern which already indicate a favourable context. Thus Forrest (1979, 65) notes the blurring of public and private interest, in this case suggesting comparisons as much with the 'old corruption' as with the colonial period, the supremacy of executive over legislature (66), and an atmosphere of secrecy and centralisation (93). He notes in particular the weakness of the scrutiny of the public service by parliament (67) and the fact that the public service in the strict sense, those bound by the Public Service Act, made up only 13% of those working for government (80). An insider view of the period prior to the public exposure phase is provided by McCarrey, formerly head of the West Australian Treasury: 'corruption begins well before the stage of monetary kickbacks ... in any retreat from principles of fairness, equity and the integrity of government decision makers' (McAdam and O'Brien, 1987, 228).

The phenomenon of the marketisation of the public service – in the form of short term contracts – is also commented on by Hughes (1998, 398) in the corruption context: 'when everyone is a contractor there is no ethos beyond the terms of the contract'. The Burke administration appointed about two hundred and fifty advisers in its first eighteen months (O'Brien, 1988, 4-5). One memorable phrase encapsulates the situation: 'the greatest possible happiness ... for those with the greatest voice' (74), an obviously favourable climate for corruption, a new utilitarianism. Weller (1974, 41) sums matters up as 'an inappropriately close relationship between government and business'. Finally as Clark noted (Clark *et al.*, 1997, 6) the image of government in West Australia and also Queensland became rather similar to that of the private sector.

As political corruption developed on such a base so also it developed particular characteristics. Matthews (Clark, *et al.*, 1997, 111-2) describes the situation thus: 'a pervasive failure by individual practitioners to observe the established proprieties, and by institutions to uphold and enforce them'. Labour came to power but a Labour party anxious to encourage the business community, a community which therefore from a starting position of being listened to attained considerable influence, often circumventing due process, and eventually in some cases power. It was contemptuous of a parliament which sat less, dealt with fewer questions, and handled official enquiries in secret (O'Brien, 1988, 17). Not all discussion uses the word corruption and direct bribery may in fact have been rare. Disproportionate payments, favouritism, and commitment of public money without a policy but with a party political rationale (Tiffen, 1999, 24-6) were not, and in the end the state government found itself underwriting three of its favoured enterprises, most notably Rothwell's Bank, to the tune of 20% of state revenue and in excess of $A600 million (O'Brien, 1988, 9). West Australia unlike Queensland and as had been forecast by O'Brien (1986, xiii) had become a largely unsuccessful corporate state especially in the domains of land and resource development. More traditionally connexions, laced no doubt with friendship and support, gave certain businesses an unfair and irrational edge, as in the case of the proposed replacement of an abattoir by a brickworks, over their less favoured competitors (McAdam and O'Brien, 1987, xv). Among other examples of favouritism O'Brien (1988, 9) notes Argyle Diamonds, Fremantle Gas and Coke, the Anchorage Project, the Swan Brewery site and the Perth tech site. Note the frequency of development land in this context.

The ensuing crash, when the economic as well as the political climate turned against such activities was as much financial as political. Heads wobbled and in a number of cases rolled. Significant sums of money were wasted and not available for other purposes. Corruption made a difference – for the worse on any kind of cost-benefit analysis – of a kind scarcely supportive of any benevolent or functionalist account of corruption. Corruption however was exposed and acted upon in a less clear cut and conspicuous fashion than in Queensland. The eventual public enquiry tended to downplay corruption, while yet referring to it in a confidential appendix, and recognising deep public concern over standards of political behaviour (Weller, 1994, 47-51). The state government avoided full implementation of its recommendations (Weller, 1994, 54). It should be noted at this stage that Costigan and Fitzgerald's enquiries and 'West Australia Inc' were the most spectacular and controversial among several such (Tiffen, 1999, 93-6; Weller, 1994) and enjoyed significant if not complete success. Others which may have had similar potential were inadequate, ignored or manipulated (Tiffen, 1999, 99-101). It is however the case that both states now provide abundant examples and a relatively favourable climate for in depth research of a kind which would have been impossible and unthinkable even a decade ago.

At the other extreme, and predictably, neither South Australia nor Tasmania provide examples of spectacular corruption of the kind which took over government in Queensland and West Australia. The occasional alleged examples were environmental and parliamentary in Tasmania, and financial in South Australia. In the South Australian case, the problems of the State Bank of South Australia and its over rapid expansion, inefficiency and inability appear more appropriate evaluations than corruption, a significant difference from what might be said in West Australia and Victoria (Clarke, 351-2). Less conspicuously the continuance of the older tradition of a modest level of corruption, well entrenched but scarcely peculiar to Australia in general, is documented in the local press and in the South Australian case by the police anti-corruption branch which investigates all public sector corruption. The establishment in 1989 of such a branch in a state with a generally good reputation and six years after the first initiatives is indicative of changes in public and political attitudes (Cornish, 1998). Its focus is on serious corruption – organised, systematic, long term, substantial – and in discussing causes it emphasises the traditional code of silence (the low probability of being caught) and a weak staff rotation policy which allows long service in one place. As to Tasmania, where a member was bribed – $110000 and the promise of the Legislative Council speakership – to cross the floor, this appears to be one of the rare cases where the individual attitudes of one individual – premier Gray – were of paramount importance. It is also interesting to note that he was found to have converted political donations to personal use in some cases, i.e. he took his cut (Clarke, 1989, 357-8).

The reasons for this situation suggest themselves, the backwater status of the island state, the tradition of honest government in South Australia in a context of unspectacular development enhanced by the removal of the country's most spectacular gerrymander. What Tasmania does provide at the start of this period is the setting for a powerful and convincing – and I suspect little known – analysis of political corruption (Hay, 1977), an analysis incomplete and highly particular but also widely applicable. It will be returned to for a fuller discussion at a later point.

There remain for discussion Victoria and New South Wales – in this context Tasmania and South Australia writ large, or Queensland and West Australia in a central location with a longer history? Although Victoria was the starting point for Costigan neither state has provided a public spectacle of Queensland or West Australian style or dimensions. A cynic however might venture the comment that everyone knew they were like that anyway. Thus police corruption was a long standing problem in both states, closely connected with 'vice'. It is alleged that much unreported corruption occurred and that in several ways investigation was problematic.

The extent of corruption in New South Wales was a matter of continuous controversial debate in the 1970s and 1980s (Tiffen, 1999, 133). Steketee and Cockburn (1986, 292-3) regarded the phenomenon as a bipartisan non-issue in New South Wales in the early 1980s though they note the development ethos of this period (187). Premier Wran's position was to dismiss charges of corruption as isolated and inevitable (253), and as part of the traditional political armoury of accusation and abuse. By 1984 an experienced public administrator could comment that 'it is difficult to escape the impression that corruption has become widespread' (Alaba, 1994, 80-1) but the government nevertheless won the next state election. In the mid 1980s a Royal Commission (Steketee and Wran, 1989, 292-328) cleared Wran of accusations of interference in the judicial process. However, Wran's cynicism was eventually damaging (336). The observation by Terrill (1987, 105) that corruption was more general in the more entrepreneurial Sydney than in Melbourne might well be discounted, coming as it did from the editor of *The Age*, Melbourne's daily.

Wran had no conspicuous contemporary in Melbourne although the vigorous development tradition of city and state never disappeared. Certainly in the land and housing development boom of the 1970s there is evidence in Victoria (Victoria, 1978 (1)) that both at state and local government level corruption was endemic as revealed by both official and other explorations. There were also strong suspicions of the misuse for private gain by legislators and officials of information acquired in the course of their public duties (Sandercock, 1975, 232-8). The strongly pro-development policies of the administration of premier Kennett (1992-99) have generated vigorous accusations of corruption focused on ways and means used via a series of large and controversial projects to reshape the city's identity. At this point the intellectual wealth and imagination of the public response becomes evident, a response which places Australia at the sharp end of current discussion and debate.

The tradition of incisive and original reflexion on the subject is nothing new. It is at least a century old, rivalled only in North America. Within the period under scrutiny in the early 1980s a Victorian cabinet minister comes up with the interesting idea of crime impact statements for proposed legislation – how vulnerable to corruption (and crime) is what is proposed? – as well as the idea of a National Corruption Authority though neither has been implemented (Bottom, 1987, 107). Gray's (1991) study of a country town notes that local opinion connects corruption and centralisation (99) and explores the means alternative to corruption whereby the powerful get their own way which means may reasonably be assumed to be widespread. A thoroughly intellectual response to Kennett's programme in Victoria has come from Logan's team at Deakin University (Johnson, Logan and Long, 1999) arguing that Kennett's policy is essentially post-modernist in its fragmentation, its eschewal and denial of the meta-narratives which underlie the planning process and their concomitant of rational resource allocation. He would go so far as to argue that a post-modernist position inevitably denies the validity of the idea of public interest and thus of conflict of interest intrinsic in the idea of political corruption. Finally the claim is made that the very structure of government has been changed to legalise or extend the legal domain of favouritism, raising implicitly the question hardly touched upon here of the status of political corruption under bad or partisan laws.

Logan raises important and troubling intellectual questions and considerable real world stumbling blocks. The New South Wales Independent Commission Against Corruption (ICAC) has for a decade provided not only practical solutions in the domain of investigation and action but also a well considered intellectual position on a range of central issues. As the country's leading such authority, and in its potentially exemplary role, it deserves discussion in its own right, a discussion facilitated by its wide and accessible range of publications.

On the substantive side ICAC (ICAC, 1989-; ICAC, 1995-) provides an account of more than ten years of activity against corruption (or more exactly reported corruption) in the state.[1] The spectrum of activity is broad and for the most part familiar – land-use, building inspection, patronage, speed money, police, and most recently (at the time of writing) racing and stolen cars. However there are surprising and novel dimensions. The state railway system has been looked at on three occasions and appears highly corruption tolerant (ICAC, 1998 (1)). Among areas involved are carriage cleaning contracts, favouritism and sale of commercially sensitive information. Given that the ICAC sample was 'only a very small fraction' a quantitative estimate is impossible, but loss or theft and sale of materials alone was about half a million dollars. More happily ICAC has met with some success in the sensitive area of operation of Aboriginal Land Councils at the request of aggrieved aboriginals. Here the central issues were not land itself but favouritism and conflict of interest together with general maladministration. ICAC has also had to investigate false accusations of corruption against councillors and officials by solicitors, developers and planners (ICAC, 1997 (4)).

In terms of prosecution roughly half the cases bought by ICAC have been proven but of course not all complaints – in fact a small proportion – proceed to that point. In some instances the development of preventive measures is more appropriate – corruption proofing – the problem of boat moorings and ferry tickets in Sydney Harbour for example (ICAC, 1992 (1)). And most fundamental is the generation of changes in attitude and ethos. This is of course impossible to measure but in its 1996-7 Annual Report (7) ICAC is able to note that 'a number of significant investors ... have commented on the difference in doing business here compared with other Australian states'.

This is not just a matter of well publicised success in particular cases but of the use of such cases to develop discussion of more basic issues as well as papers focused in that area, underpinned by an informed understanding of the history of corruption in the state. Three instances illuminate this situation. A report on local government in 1992 (ICAC, 1992 (2)) identifies pecuniary interest of members and a particular form of conflict of interest (where councils both own land and regulate its use as the planning authority) as key issues. The substantive basis is that one thousand of the complaints to ICAC in its first three years, a third of the total, related to local government, and three quarters of these to planning and development. Over one hundred – more than half – of the state's local councils were affected. As to pecuniary interest, ICAC suggests a specialist tribunal reserving criminal charges only for extreme cases (bribery included). As to conflict of interest ICAC rejects the often advanced proposal that the real estate trade should be debarred from elected office, preferring careful monitoring and special rules with respect to the relationship with professional staff. The starting point is a councillor's comment (15): 'if you exclude the business people and the people with perhaps the know-how and an understanding of the area, you're not going to get good members to join councils'. This situation is of course neither new nor peculiarly municipal: it could equally well have been made in terms of colonial legislatures.

An early report in this area was on North Coast Land Development (1990). This enquiry brought confrontation with lawyers and parliamentarians. The vehemence of ICAC's statements given that it is a lawyer dominated body must have come as a surprise. The outcome, with characteristic Australian directness, is to state fundamental issues. In response to a developer's lawyer's comments likening a lawyer's work to a lobbyist's ICAC remarks: 'there is a difference between paying a lawyer to argue your case and paying the lawyer for an introduction to the judge – or to an influential friend of the judge' (650). In the same report ICAC comments 'bribery is a well known English word. Most people know what it means. Only the law has difficulty with it' (615). On another occasion: 'the fundamental right of all citizens to equality of treatment in the hands of public officials' (655) is noted, and in the same context a comment from an 1883 enquiry on the public lands is likewise quoted: 'the rights and interests of all have been the sport of accident, political interest and departmental disorder' (xi). The same enquiry is quoted in the report's introduction (xi): 'self-interest has created a laxity of conscience ... the stain attaches to men of all classes and all degrees'. Some of the discussion is distinctively Australian in substance as well as style, the relationship – if any – between mateship and cronyism (651). On the substantive side the 1990 enquiry revealed that from 1982 a property and development consultancy had paid councillors and officials to provide information and to influence decisions in such areas as zoning, building height regulations and resort development. It is interesting to note that the sums involved were small, typically in the range $5-10000 by comparison with the scale of the projects (Chapter 6). This did not remain the case: by 1997 such figures as $60000 to a building inspector, $20000 to abort a demolition order on a defective building, and $10-20000 to expedite a controversial approval are reported (ICAC, 1997 (5), 9-23). Queensland Criminal Justice Commission cases of the same period (Queensland CJC, 1991) as the New South Wales North Coast Enquiry and of a similar kind also indicate a higher payment level at least in aggregate.

A 1991 investigation, again of land development and allegations that a member of the legislature had required a bribe, led to a proposed code of conduct for members in which the existing oath, simply of allegiance, would be replaced by one which also covered duties and responsibilities

(ICAC, 1991 (1), 1). The interesting precedent of a 1923 case when attempts to prosecute a member for accepting a bribe to put pressure on the Minister for Lands failed because 'the charge did not disclose an offence known to law' is discussed and again indicates the long standing nature of the problem. This report also discusses the regulation of lobbyists.

The scale of ICAC's operations has been huge. The fact that in its first two years ICAC received more than 2000 complaints tells us a great deal about political corruption in the state in 1990 (ICAC, 1991 (1), 5). From these it identified nineteen issues which can be further collapsed into five areas: hospitality; contracts and tenders; the party political element; administrative culture; and the legal framework. On a different scale local government accounts for about one third of complaints; police, aboriginal land, corrective services each for 7%-8% and no other single category much in excess of 3.3%. If ICAC changed community attitudes – roughly half of those surveyed see corruption as a major problem – it has not found it easy to obtain enthusiastic bureaucratic cooperation in some areas, notably whistleblower protection. Much of this is not new. The ICAC approach to it is. That it has not been widely emulated is a matter of regret but sadly not of surprise.

This is the first and at least in part positive point to make in summarising the contemporary situation. One state has shown the way, Queensland has followed, the rest have not. The obvious explanation, but not the only one, is that the ICAC style and substance comes too close for the comfort of state politicians, officials, some lawyers and business interests. A second positive point is that public interest has not only been roused but altered, not simply by ICAC but by a wider range of investigations and their findings during two decades. The scale and consequences of the outcomes of corruption have been the prime factor. That scale has been in part the result of the internationalisation even globalisation of corruption. Of course local and petty corruption remains but big business on a global scale has become the dominant player. It will receive less sympathy and tolerance from the Australian public than the local version. The obverse of this situation is to note for how long and to what extent corrupt operators were able to carry public opinion with them, the intelligent as well as the ignorant. It was only when either corruption became blatant and conspicuously greedy or when the wheels came off that the situation changed. Advice to the would-be corrupt: maintain a modest life style and eschew risky large scale exercises! But can the present more favourable climate of public opinion and political action be sustained? The attractions of corruption remain and will not simply go away. Maintenance of public vigilance and even of effectively independent institutions to counter corruption cannot be readily assumed or easily guaranteed. A best case scenario envisages entrenchment of a radically changed popular view – broad based intolerance – via effective institutions, both those formally dedicated to this end and the political machine in general – in brief a changed political culture. The worst case is of both a relapse towards general tolerance and the gradual emasculation of institutions such as ICAC. In this area the old Public Service Boards provide an unhappy precedent. The required positive change in political culture turns out to be broader than at first expected, a true accountability rather than the cosmetic bureaucratic monster which has so often assumed its name while destroying its meaning. Our questions and speculations are then to be answered not only in terms of the particularities of Australia's experience of political corruption over two centuries but also in terms of Australians' understandings and interpretations of the phenomenon. Even if it is a phenomenon which Australians have generally taken for granted, with or without regret, rather than explored and evaluated in a formal sense there is material for discussion. Where does it fit, what brought about this situation, what does it tell us about Australia? These are all worthwhile questions and if they are not addressed any examination of political corruption in Australia will be incomplete. That path to completion is the role of the final part of this work.

Note

1   ICAC is a prolific publisher: its publications are available from ICAC, GPO Box 500, Sydney, NSW 2001, Australia. The bibliography lists a sample of important recent work.

7 Causes and Characteristics

A brief empirical account of Australia's experience of political corruption will be incomplete not simply on account of its brevity or of problems of evidence or method but because it will fall short on such issues as cause, character and consequences. While discussion of these central issues must be evidence based it is too much to expect the evidence always to speak for itself. It is also too much to expect more than limited consensus: rival but neither unrelated nor wholly incompatible interpretations are in order.

Broad Perspectives

An essential preliminary in this context is to place Australian political corruption in perspective. It has never been shown with any credibility that Australia been taken over by corruption save locally and ephemerally. Even at those scales its power was contested both at the time and in subsequent accounts. For whatever reason it was generally more possible and more likely that the immigrant or native born would do better by active involvement in the productive economy in Australia than as a rent seeking instrument or agent of venality. This was much less true of for example Latin America for reasons and with consequences well known but beyond the scope of this book (Andreski, 1966, 80-1; 104-5). Much the same can be said of post-colonial Africa. In Australia the more favourable situation was both underpinned by and contributed to democratic institutions and a degree of egalitarianism though again there is a rich diversity of interpretation. If the significance of political corruption is at times overstated in Australia the twin risks of reductionism – of placing corruption in the middle – or more dangerously and more probably of residualism – its invocation as explanation of the otherwise inexplicable – are relatively slight.

Corruption is part of the broad political process, an understated and intrinsically and deliberately obscure part but only a part. The danger here is of simplistic juxtaposition with good competent and honest government. This latter version has never been the whole story any more than has corruption. There are the neglected dimensions of muddle, mishap and incompetence which are not the same as corruption, but which are easily confused with it and good ground for its cultivation. Like corruption they are rarely studied in their own right, providing no more than a modest counterpoint in mainstream accounts of political institutions. The danger is that since the outcomes are often similar – delay in process, higher costs and manifestly poor decisions for example – the two different processes will be inadequately differentiated.

Where is political corruption to be located within Australian culture? Its existence is indisputable – but is it woven inexorably and inextricably into what is now a very distinctive way of life? The reason for these questions will be more obvious to anyone who has looked at corruption on a global scale. Scrutiny of third world corruption always raises the question and defence that 'this is how we do it, have always done it' (and plan to carry on doing it). In dictatorships and authoritarian regimes in general corruption is so integral to the nature of government as to be inevitable. In either case it is central to the political culture and to question it is to address fundamentals. Corruption enjoys no such centrality in Australia. Few Australians would respond to particular instances of corruption in terms of 'the way we do it' or would accept, even reluctantly, that political corruption should be recognised as an integral part of Australian culture.[1] If the more reflective might admit to temptation the majority do not succumb and the preference for a global reputation as an honest country is general. And that is the greater part of Australia's reputation (and culture) with the qualification however that international image understandably understates the state and municipal dimension of the country's political life. Even in a decade of much increased media exposure political corruption is not the everyday experience of every Australian and the wish is that things will stay that way even if Australians are uncertain and inconstant in their efforts to achieve this objective.

The context this provides for a discussion of cause, character and consequence is then one of consensus as to where corruption belongs in Australia – preferably it does not – but disagreement on many of the details as to where it resides and what should be done. And here the matter of the misuse of the very word receives essential reiteration. The existence of a still widespread complacency, and of course of an active minority whose political culture is corrupt and venal, cannot be gainsaid. The former feature has certainly diminished. Australia at present appears less complacent and less tolerant in this area than almost any other country and better informed as to both the facts and the underlying issues. We are discussing a modern open democracy, not perfection but surely a 'lucky country', in which nevertheless corruption is present reality as well as past experience. Why, what, and whither?

Causes

Tasmania as a Case Study

The most stimulating and thoughtful account of the causal dimension of Australian political corruption is Hay's 1977 paper in the New Zealand journal *Political Science* (115-30). Quite apart from the relative obscurity of its location its other limitations are obvious: it is about Tasmania, hardly the mainstream of Australian politics or political corruption, and has a contemporary focus. It remains nevertheless a seminal piece which ought to be better known. Hay argues five basic causes for political corruption: behavioural expectations imposed by law but not shared by society at large; rapid social change; size of political unit; the level of ideological content in political activity; and inequalities. The second and fifth of these he regards as inapplicable to contemporary Tasmania, but they certainly can be applied to Tasmania's past as well as to several other Australian states past and present. As to expectations Hay cites five examples since 1945, one internal to parliament, four external, and all involving bribes. The argument convinces and its wider applicability is obvious and ubiquitous. In more general terms he argues that many Tasmanians enter public and political life without accepting the behavioural norms which a Westminster system assumes. Again this is no Tasmanian peculiarity. Arguably its most disturbing conclusion, based on several case studies, is the degree to which at least until the 1970s involved parties and the public at large saw little wrong with what was happening.

On the question of size Hay explores the infrequently discussed question of the 'too small' case. (Bennett (1992) elsewhere (31) argues a similar case in much more general terms.) This impinges upon the first of his causes: are there enough able people in Tasmania? To this he would add the informality of Tasmanian politics, and high costs in the absence of economies of scale. Informality is a valued, long standing and beneficial dimension of Australian culture, not merely political culture. In a more wide ranging account of Australian state politics Bennett (1992) comments upon the importance of informal influence in a small scale political order. But it is also the case that good government requires some formality. Hyde's condemnation of 'government by wink, nod and handshake' as corrupt comes to mind (Clark *et al.*, 1997, 70-1) as a telling description. As to costs Hay is able to point out important gaps and consequences: no

Hansard at the time he was writing, though one was promised; a small parliament with an often tiny government back bench. Both of these situations favour corruption.

In his fifth point Hay argues that in the absence of ideology Tasmanian politics becomes the politics of what works – the functionalist approach – and thus of brokerage and of wheeling and dealing. The alternative position that equates ideology with high motives and principles put into unimpeachable practice may again be overdrawn but the point deserves consideration. Interestingly two prominent American scholars writing two decades later also link corruption and ideology in a comparable way, seeing 'a political class motivated ... by ideology ... displaced by individuals who view politics primarily as business' (della Porta and Vannucci, 1999, 85).

The two points put aside by Hay also require discussion. Tasmania scarcely epitomises rapid social change until one considers the advent of the convicts when it becomes a legitimate albeit unusual approach. Recall that Van Diemen's Land was proverbially venal. Extended to the mainland the argument carries great force, the corruption of colonial Victoria and contemporary Queensland for example. The connexion is also of course one that is to be observed globally, in New World cities in the second half of the nineteenth century and much of the contemporary and especially the urban third world.

Gross inequality of wealth as an explanation can be dumbed down into an explanation of corruption in terms of poverty, a traditional and limited account often with a hidden agenda of inhibiting wide debate. But if the concept of inequality is extended from wealth to include status, power and rights it becomes even more credible, powerful and wide ranging. It is part of any account of political corruption in convict Australia, or even the whole if the 'old corruption' be reinterpreted in terms of inequality. It clearly underlies the corruption associated with land settlement in every one of the colonies – the squatter/settler confrontation – and also, albeit to a lesser degree, the land development corruption of recent decades. Indeed the danger is of its over-extension to the point of vacuousness. However as Corbett (Clark *et al.*, 1997, 32-3) has recently pointed out increasing inequality (of wealth) can be connected to the ethical malaise – of which corruption is part – not only in contemporary Australian politics, but also to a long standing body of political thought on the subject. Likewise an anonymous editorialist (Anon, 1981) in the *Australian and New Zealand Journal of Criminology* clearly favours class over alternatives focused either on morality or simply coping.

In brief Hay has provided an excellent springboard from which he himself has made several very good plunges. But he has the limitations of a solo virtuoso diver, unrecognised and unapplauded he has swum on to 'fresh fields and pastures new' leaving the 'deep end' but limitedly explored.

Personality and Morality

To propose an alternative account to that of Hay is not then to question rather it is to augment and fill out. The traditional starting point for any exploration of the causes of political corruption is personality and individual morality. It is a dangerous and difficult position for several reasons. It is the position typically adopted by those who wish to divert attention from the structural and general and thus to avoid awkward questions challenging the established order. Even without this dimension it strongly particularises explanation, a proto-post-modernism. To be moralistic adds little to our understanding. If however such an account is broadened out from the personal to the public it is considerably empowered. Political corruption is an expression of both the private *and* public moral condition not only in itself but also in the reactions it engenders, complacent acceptance, witch-hunt or searching questions. Neither condition alone is a sufficient account. When that has been said it must never be forgotten that corruption only happens when there are men and women willing to cheat, lie and steal, to transact political business in an immoral fashion. This is the case even when we make allowances for petty corruption, recognising the greater moral turpitude of the extortionist, and for the evasion of bad laws, the moral responsibility of the legislator. There is no escaping the fact that political corruption is an intrinsically moral issue.

'Old Corruption' and New Corruption

The move forward in the Australian context is to look at the moral condition of each of the four phases around which our empirical account is structured: convict, colonial, Commonwealth and contemporary. That the convict period provided an enduring component of Australia's political culture is widely accepted. The wisest account of this phenomenon focuses not on individuals but on a system which was for at least several decades a manifestation of the 'old corruption'. The character of the penal population has if anything been more controversial than that of the system. Governor Macquarie commented as unfavourably on the free as on the unfree part of his flock: 'those who had been sent out here and those who ought to have been' (1907-9, 309). In brief the initial human raw material might have been expected to raise problems of governance in any circumstance. Add a context of 'old corruption' in general and the surprise is that penal Australia was not more corrupt. Hancock (1930, 41) rightly emphasises the elusiveness of its ongoing influence, a point taken up in terms of its persistence by a perceptive journalist in an *Economist* survey (7 March 1987). Crowley (1971, 14), writing of Forrest, the first premier of West Australia, notes that convictism while not the cradle of Australian politics provided an atmosphere of 'crime, punishment and authoritarian government' which influenced public political attitudes just at the period when Australian nationalism was born. All three are wiser and shrewder than the simplistic versions still occasionally encountered. The component with the most readily discernible momentum is patronage, witness the problems of public service reform achieved only incompletely and impermanently in the years around 1900. Patronage has reinvented itself in the propensity of modern state governments to run down the traditional public service in favour of a larger group of political appointees. It should in fairness be added that what replaced patronage, essentially seniority, guarantees neither overall effectiveness nor freedom from corruption. And as Russell (Clark *et al.*, 162-3) notes the public service boards never wholly lost their interest in administrative ethics.

'Old corruption' is rarely explored from a moral perspective. By comparison the morality of the convicts and of the emigrant stream of free settlers who, from about 1830, overwhelmed it was often so discussed. The discussion in the 1990s and for the foreseeable future focuses primarily on the seizure of land from the indigenous peoples though rarely as an act of corruption. The traditional critique ignores this point in almost every case and looks rather at the background of the convicts and the ambitions of the settlers, ambitions to be satisfied primarily in material terms whether on the land, in the mines, or in the cities and towns. Material success was not only accorded a high status by individuals and the community, but was viewed as at least compatible with, at worst central to, a whole corpus of attitudes, ideas and opinions, a secular as well as religious theology which marginalised the weak, the unsuccessful and the inconvenient and which possessed a low view of social justice. A surprisingly large number of contemporaries emphasise that immigrant Scots were especially prone to move into this position in which acts of corruption lost their immoral connotation (Murphy and Joyce, 1978, 127). Crowley (1971), offering an alternative, or complement, follows his observations on the tendency of the settler to look to the government for everything (13-4), with a perceptive account of the implications of the transplantation of the ethos of the

English public school to Australia for the purposes of élite education (19). The particular context is Forrest's education at Bishop Hale's School Perth. In his view the emphasis placed on community leadership rather than individual rights and its acceptance of inequality was pernicious. He sets out on, though he never fully explores, a trail with a considerable potential for incorporation in any causal and contextual account of Australian political corruption, and an interesting counterpoint to the more widely articulated evaluations of the role of Presbyterian individualism.

A third strand of discussion connects corruption and Roman Catholicism or more exactly Irish Catholicism. This has often been more a matter of popular opinion and prejudice than of considered reflection, but cannot be dismissed – any more than the other two categories – as mere bigotry. The best discussion, in Brennan's (1971) biography of John Wren, is concerned to explore, as well it must be admitted to try to justify, the distinctive role of Catholics in Australia's political corruption and the extent to which that appellation is justified.

Bureaucracy

Australia was *ab initio* an extremely bureaucratic and highly regulated society. Political corruption presupposes a degree of both. The peculiar relationship between colonial settler and government was only one facet, and a relatively short lived one, of the regulated government-citizen relationship which was the domain of political corruption. That corruption did not depend on any particular set of regulations. Even as land settlement wound down and state governments finally established a workable legal framework – for land corruption in the colonial period had thrived on badly constructed and indifferently administered legislation – new spheres emerged. Both global wars were fought at least on the home front by regulation, so too was the war against the economic depression of the 1930s by governments of both parties and so too was post-war recovery managed, especially in the areas of land-use planning and resource management. These are not all areas notable for indifferent legislation. Rather they represent Hay's first category of expectations not matched by society generally or in this case even more importantly by particular and often powerful individuals. Alongside this must be placed the epidemics of municipal corruption in the Commonwealth period in which weakness of the regulatory apparatus was conspicuously present.

Corruption can be located not only in the substance of government but its style. The case for and against the inevitability of government activism in colonial settlement can be argued to and fro but in the Australian case there was gravitation towards activism, on the basis of the convict antecedent and environmental conditions. From Governor King onwards Australian government has dealt in detail – and been overwhelmed by it – right through to at least the 1990s, a recipe for corruption. The nature of the Commonwealth exacerbated this situation concentrating attention at state level upon the fine print of service delivery, a bridge here, a hospital there, the disbursement of funds and favours. Simultaneously the size of Australia, the nature of its developmental problems, and the small size of the population made it inevitable that discretionary powers would in fact be widely dispersed even while excessive centralisation was widely held responsible for corruption, and decentralisation advocated as a solution (Prasser *et al.*, 1990, 235-6). In other words a curious combination of local discretion, excessive centralisation and hands on activism provided a favourable climate. Government grew in a direction favourable for corruption, middle-heavy.

For most of Australia's history the economic and social context in which government and bureaucracy operated has been developmental, a growing population and economy in need of at least some order and control, that order and control conflicting with the wishes and hopes of particular groups and individuals to whom corruption was a way round the impasse. This situation was further complicated by unsatisfactory legislation – not surprisingly so given the unusual and unfamiliar dimension of the Australian experience – and the scarcity of skilled personnel. The environmental element certainly deserves emphasis at this point, superficially and misleading similar to Britain but in reality both different and difficult. Much regulation to protect the settler from himself served equally albeit inadequately to protect the environment from the settler, and corruption served simply for the degradation of both.

Mateship

To what extent does the well known if elusive idea of 'mateship' provide a distinctively Australian element to this discussion. Pilger (1989, chapter 6) gives it a very central role. In the strict sense the idea is of bonding, essentially male bonding, born of adverse experience, especially as pioneer or soldier. In a broader sense it might be applied to the close and lasting friendships made in small communities. The argument has certainly been advanced that mateship underpins various forms of corruption, cronyism and more generally favouritism as opposed to a more directly mercenary corruption. Mateship also carries a connotation of reciprocity and mutuality, a reminder of the wisdom of viewing corruption as a connected network rather than a series of disparate incidents. It is, as MacKenzie points out (1962, 109) a matter of trust, potentially a rival or alternative to that political trust which is a foundation of responsible citizenship. Mateship is only too easily exaggerated and romanticised and is of course impossible to measure. It is also too easily dismissed as history, myth or both. The social context of Australian communities, especially in rural areas, provides a rich vein of close durable friendship which can scarcely be excluded from an examination of corruption especially of that most elusive variety the small scale, local and petty. It is scarcely a factor to be invoked in the urban big business domain of the last two decades. To call those bands of thieves bribers and rule benders 'mates' would be to prostitute an honourable and useful concept. One last point: mateship is not quite uniquely Australian. It is a term equally applicable in New Zealand where the evidence suggests that political corruption is and was much less widespread than in Australia, a warning against over emphasis.

Party Politics

Most of the issues so far discussed have a long history. There remain to be examined two of more particularly recent significance. Neither political parties nor the concept of public interest, already touched upon, are new, but certain transformations in them appear very closely related to the recent Australian experience. Political corruption does not need parties – just politics. It has even been argued with some success that strong parties act against corruption even though the role of parties in generating corruption has also been convincingly argued and is more evidently conspicuous. Similarly but less strongly contested is the question as to whether or not long periods of tenure of office by one party inevitably lead to corruption (Pringle, 1958, 51-2): my answer would be a qualified yes. The novel dimension, not peculiarly Australian, is that over the last two or three decades party politics has become very expensive, especially in terms of elections and the media. Traditional means of finance became inadequate and the party turns more and more to or is sought out by wealthy patrons. Nothing new, except when the demands of the patron cross the line separating acceptable demands – general policies as spelled out in manifestoes – from the unacceptable – particular favours agreed in secret. (It should also be noted, and has less often received publicity, that such deals generally contain a large personal 'gift' alongside the political.) The divide may be conceptually essential but the nature of the evidence – note *inter alia* secrecy – makes its application difficult. Nevertheless there is good reason to believe that corruption of this kind has greatly increased in recent decades in Australia, as part of a wider issue which has moved to a more central position in political debate: how is party political activity to be financed?

The Public Interest

The concept of the public interest and its relationship not only to private interest *strictu sensu* but to a variety of sectional, local and particular interests is central to any discussion of political corruption. It has been present in Australia from the very beginning, in the confusion of such interests in the 'old corruption'. It never quite disappeared in the difficult exercise of its defence in the period of economic and geographic expansion. Its existence has rarely been challenged. Is this still the case? Can it be argued that both the politics of the market – classical Thatcherism – with its emphasis on individual and market, its denial of community, destroys or denies the idea of the public interest, and thus of political corruption. For a public interest made up of the aggregate of disparate and often competing private interests is vacuous. From a less practically political and economic focus post-modernism sets out to destroy the idea of meta-narrative, the big picture. Is the public interest such a meta-narrative, as a recent work on contemporary Victorian politics would suggest? (Johnson, Logan and Long, 1998). Many post-modernists would not share this view. Thus Heller and Fehér (1988) present an argument accommodating social justice and political corruption within a post-modernist framework. However, in more practical terms a post-modern politics dismissive of public interest in favour of the sectional, the particular, and not too worried about corruption – just another way of doing politics, on the left as well as the right – remains a frightening and, ironically, peculiarly modern possibility.

Characteristics

To attempt to characterise corruption is simultaneously to summarise the evidence, to assess its significance and to provide a necessary antidote to the universal tendency to exaggeration – to boil down what is usually blown up. The most obvious point to be made here is the traditional and ongoing centrality of land and resources (mining largely excepted) as might be expected in a recently settled country apparently rich in both. While it is also true that there is a long history of backhanders in the area of government contracts the percentage take and the overall consequences do not appear to rank alongside land and resources. Electoral corruption was once commonplace, but usually at a low level and often in the form of personation (not always, as noted, illegal). It has not quite disappeared. Petty corruption was endemic in the convict period but this century has seen it substantially restricted to the municipal level. The citizen does not generally expect to bribe or be bribed in his/her most everyday dealings with state or federal government.

Bribery is sometimes characterised as Australia's corruption of last resort (Davis, 1960, 614): by contrast more typical and prevalent were favouritism (and reciprocity), nepotism, patronage and more or less secret commissions. The denial of the most directly monetary form may be an exaggeration, a wish to stress the modernity of Australian politics. It also ignores the point that a deal of corruption where money does not change hands but a decision is altered can readily be translated into money terms, the advantage of proximity to a railway station or even of not having personally to support an army of unemployed friends and relations. There is also a tendency to ignore the essentially financial character of commissariat corruption and to marginalise it, as *exotica economica*, from the mainstream. The marginalisation of the bribe tells us as much of what Australians think about themselves as it does about Australian political corruption. It does however lead to discussion of two more important areas.

In colonial Australia in particular much corruption might be and was described as 'roads and bridges' – I would add railways and public works – characterising one of the core processes of the politics of the period. How far and how much of it can be accommodated within our definition – or any respectable definition – of corruption remains a matter of debate. Of course there were instances of bribery, and there were the cases where members (and their friends) used political power primarily to ensure their own commercial benefit. Corruption and conflict of interest is an apt description in each case. However, the legislator arguing for and supporting his electorate's case for a bridge or a road was doing his job, even if we allow the limitations and shortcomings of this process of allocation and know that he would benefit personally from particular outcome. Parkes (146) viewed this process as 'public money voted away by private pressure'. But in this area at least the idea of corruption is fuzzy rather than clear cut. The crucial questions are of method and motive, neither of which are easily explored. It is a domain of primarily historical interest even though lawyers still try to mobilise it in areas where it is not applicable. Recall too that much of what went on in Bjelke-Petersen's Queensland might be described as 'roads and bridges' writ large.

Characterisation invites comparison. Where does Australia stand internationally? With respect to the past the answer is necessarily impressionistic: penal Australia at worst perfected at best moderated an externally imposed corruption – and there is of course almost nowhere to compare it with! Colonial Australia compares favourably with both Americas and less so with New Zealand and perhaps Canada. An initial impression that during the first two-thirds of the twentieth century Australia had a seemingly ineradicable if generally low level core of corruption at state and local level which compared unfavourably with Britain or New Zealand might not stand up to close scrutiny. Britain was not looking very hard – Australia was developing the habit of doing so. In any case reputation is not reality, and the former is both easier to apprehend and more liable to misuse and misunderstanding. That has been Transparency International's experience with the corruption perception index – others are proposed looking at such areas as propensity to corrupt – which ranks Australia close to the respectable top end. It is not regarded as a corrupt country in global terms, alongside several western democracies but behind Scandinavia and New Zealand. Given that Australia is not complacent in this area and is a world leader in corruption countermeasures at least in New South Wales I would be inclined to locate Australia closer to best possible practice.

Note

1   A very recent ICAC report (ICAC, 2000, 87) on 'Rebirthing motor vehicles' (i.e. registration of stolen cars) is forced to address the cultural issue because Lebanese and Filipinos were so numerous among the offenders. The important point made is that ethnic connection was one of the bases on which criminals infiltrated the vehicle licensing bureaucracy.

8   A Consequential Conclusion

Political corruption is *inter alia* concerned with intended outcomes, normally of a specific kind. The big picture is by contrast rarely part of the participant's vision, be it as practitioner or victim. Certainly the phenomenon scarcely contributes to Australia's place in the world, or to the world's estimation of Australia. It is not mentioned in a very recent *Economist* survey (9 September 2000). (By contrast a survey of Argentina (6 May 2000) has plenty to say on the subject, as does the *Economist* in looking at Latin America, the post-communist states and the Third World – in fact the larger part of the planet – in general.) When the rest of the world looks at Australia it looks at Australia's location, resources, environment and history, as well as at current issues such as the constitutional debate and the position of the aborigines. Corruption scarcely features because it is so modestly present by comparison with say Indonesia or even Italy, and historically by comparison with say the United States or Argentina. The first thing then to say about the big picture is that it is not so big after all. Comparisons with the rest of the New World are especially cogent and the role of corruption is quite reasonably invoked in explaining the different experience of Australasia by comparison with the in many respects not dissimilar southern cone of Latin America. Australasia was fortunate enough to avoid the experience and effects of Latin corruption. Two exceptions to this assessment deserve comment. Firstly in the first half of the nineteenth century Australia exemplified a political system institutionally corrupt – but it did so in insignificant isolation and in extreme peculiarity, and its momentum was particular, limited and not for export, even locally. More significantly Australia's present and recent political corruption has been internationalised, and as big multinational business contains a corrupt component so too are Australian business dealings on the global scene subject to the actuality and risk of corruption. But again Australia is not Thailand or Russia – the scale of the outcomes is modest by international standards. Australia performs on the world stage as the Commonwealth much more than the member states and as has been noted reality and repute are in this former context generally good.

However, at the meso-scale, essentially and most conspicuously the states, the results of political corruption cannot adequately be regarded as a few frayed edges. The fabric of the Australian political jacket is not rags and tatters but it is well worn in several vulnerable and conspicuous places. One evident attribute, and this is to reintroduce an historical dimension, is interstate difference, a relatively clean South Australia, an entrenched (rather than profound) tradition in the south-east, spectacular instances in the recent history of Queensland and West Australia. To generalise at this level is to aggregate local instances, more exactly known local instances, a comment which denotes qualification. When that has been said it is not unreasonable to suggest the significance of political corruption at the meso-scale in three respects: in the past the near universal conflict between pastoralist and settler and thus the whole process of rural settlement possessed a large component of corruption; large scale urban development especially in recent decades – the planning process; and most generally added cost. In each of these categories corruption made a difference. Stated thus reductionism is avoided: corruption is certainly not the whole but nor is it the residual story. As far as settlement goes environmental conditions and an evolving understanding of these clearly matter too. But the conclusion is unavoidable that resort to corruption, based on possession of appropriate resources, often enough gave the squatter an edge; the outcome over two centuries has been a more pastoral and less agricultural Australia. Likewise in urban, especially city, Australia the geography is not quite – and occasionally not at all – what wise policy and planning and its honest implementation might have provided. And it cost more, a comment made by the more sagacious and determined investigators in every generation but now at the heart of the matter. This cost is impossible to estimate but even hypothetically it is worth translating into reduced taxation or unmet needs and unimplemented possibilities.

The trouble is that so much counterfactuality in this discussion possesses the unusual defect (for such explorations) of an uncertain factual base. This problem has no perfect solution but it may be appropriate to suggest that the exploration of the personal affairs and public actions of the key groups of politicians, public servants and those whose livelihood was based on frequent interaction with them might sharpen our focus on that factual lacuna, if only to replace unlikely speculations (or none at all) with a higher level of probability. Where for example were and are the anomalous accumulations of wealth and where did they come from?

The question of cost and rationality arises not only at the meso scale, as noted, but also at the most local. Particular places and communities were thus exposed, deprived and even occasionally surprised. In much of Australia an analysis of what is where and why at the local and simple level requires a discussion not only of politics but, much harder, of the condition of those bodies politic. Again good evidence is hard to get, one reason why as already noted our understanding of political corruption in small town and rural Australia scarcely extends beyond suspicion of the substantial. There is again a pressing need for detailed case studies eschewing reductionism and attempting an empirical exploration of the place of political corruption in small communities, a formidable task.[1] My evaluation would be that vice has always possessed and will continue to possess a particularly strong local dimension, mediating as it does between highly individual demands and political regulation. Neither a selective lessening of the latter nor the introduction of a national or international element has altered this situation. Gambling and liquor have not disappeared from the vice or corruption supply scene – though they may have been relocated – and sex and drugs are not best viewed as nothing more than local representations of an essentially global phenomenon.

Finally the divergent interpretations of the place of political corruption in Australian discourse deserves comment. Characterisation must accept and accommodate this situation. Pearl, writing in 1958 of the years around 1900 was concerned that 'people do not feel very much about it when it is happening – and forget all abut it soon after' and notes how much easier it was to make a comeback in such situations in Australia than Britain. Banjo Paterson (Semmler, 1984, 138) by contrast and writing at as well as of the same period asserts an apparently opposite view: 'here (in London) a general may half wreck an empire and no one does anything; with us if a sergeant of volunteers is derated for drunkenness there is a Labour member to demand a special committee of the house to enquire into it'. The context is not of course exactly that of corruption. The point that Paterson is making, an assertion of difference in the characteristic response to political scandal in the two places once it has passed a certain threshold is however the opposite of Pearl's: 'those are the two systems and each has its drawbacks. You pay your money and don't have any choice' (138).

Approaching the Future

Alongside this kind of discussion an interpretation of Australia's historical experience must also precede speculation as to the possible futures. History must in this case be read or re-examined forward. The idea of the convict stain has certainly disappeared, at least in any crude form, from serious discussion of the Australian condition if not entirely from popular accounts or even opinion. Convict ancestry is now more likely to be celebrated rather than concealed. At least in this sense Australia has at last come to terms with its past. Here there is no need for apology. From the ongoing perspective of political corruption what is important is that for its first half century of European settlement Australia's government was an evolving mixture of the authoritarian executive, essentially penal, and the 'old corruption', quite different in its whole, though not its parts, from the experience of anywhere else, at least at so significant a spatial scale. The consensus that this laid the foundations of a very distinctive attitude towards governments, one riddled with tensions and inconsistencies, is widespread and has already been discussed. It was not an attitude grossly changed by the end of transportation and the rapid switch to representative government. In terms of individual survival and advancement it proved with modest adaptation as viable an option in the colonial era with its powerful development ethos as in the penal area when control headed the government's agenda. The same is true of the Commonwealth phase since development remained a powerful consensus, albeit intermittently interrupted, while in the new guise of states the colonies remained largely in charge of development. The genus of changes which were to become important towards the end of the Commonwealth's first century begin to appear, an international component and an increasing role and place for political parties, but the essentials remain similar to those of the colonial half century. So do evaluations and reactions: political corruption excites interest and attracts attention intermittently, when spectacular misbehaviour is exposed, but only rarely does it sustain a place on the agenda for any substantial period. Thus the anti-corruption organisation of the 1930s proved ephemeral, and even the most spectacular rorts and scams in New South Wales in the 1950s and 1960s failed to securely establish for corruption a place in either the intellectual or practical political agenda.

Two initial reasons for the beginnings of a reassessment of this interpretation in the last two decades of the twentieth century have already been given. To them must be added others: spectacular and well publicised exposures of very large scale corruption in several Australian states, often involving huge losses and misappropriation of public funds. Scale, spatial and financial, rather than form differentiated these events from their forebears; and in some instances a suspected connexion to the federal government was rather confirmed by the nature of its reaction. Conspiracy theory became credible. Simultaneously political corruption was exposed in a number of countries, most famously and influentially in Italy and very widely in the third world, in such ways and forms as to ensure its continuing presence on global political agendas and to enhance investigative processes hitherto feeble or even taboo. The end of complacency might be too robust an interpretation and the nature of media interest does not always facilitate thoughtful reaction, at worst fixing its limits scarcely beyond 'heads must roll'. Nor has it eliminated powerful forces, commonly the beneficiaries of corruption, whose realistic interest is not so much to keep corruption out of the public eye as to use their strength to thwart, stifle and subdue investigative process, a situation by no means peculiar to Australia. Nevertheless the present climate is more favourable to the minimisation of political corruption – elimination is agreed to be impossible – than for perhaps two hundred years, and Australia is better placed than most countries to seize this opportunity. How might it best be done?

Management of Corruption

Firstly to secure a permanence for present levels of interest and action and forms of institution it is necessary to accept that the present situation is a beginning. One way to ensure that it goes nowhere will be to fossilise present practices and forms, to see ICAC for example as the last word rather than the first. Given the centrality of the states to Australia's political corruption it is however quite appropriate to add that every state needs an ICAC or something like it. The same is true of the broad legal framework within which such organisations work with the addendum that the question is more often one of bringing up to date rather than of refining and retuning a reasonably adequate *status quo*.

This argument assumes the constitutional *status quo* as far as federal-state relations are concerned. This is a not unreasonable assumption given the difficulties written into the federal constitution as far as formal change is concerned though articulate advocates of a thorough revision do exist. Any revision however is unlikely to displace the meso scale regional bureaucracies which have, in the form of states, figured so prominently. Something like the states doing a similar job is bound to survive. There is probably more scope for big reforms, though not necessarily any more likelihood that they will happen, at the municipal level where in any case, especially outside metropolitan areas, our understanding is most limited even a decade down the ICAC track.

A more difficult task is to entrench and protect reforms in the direction of diverting state government away from formal and informal practices in which executive power dominated – a much more than Australian problem in early twenty-first century democracies – towards a system which couples room for action with scope for restraint and discussion. The view that executive dominance in state parliaments has fostered and facilitated corruption has received wide support, but those very supporters often relapse from such virtue when they gain power – and are corrupted by it. It makes political life so much easier! Experience suggests that securing any reform, whether with or without a new constitutional framework, will not be easy. Despite what went on in Queensland in the 1980s, Victoria's premier Kennett had no problems in implementing a strong executive version of state government in the 1990s, and changing the state's geography in the process. The fact that the electors ejected Kennett, thereby incidentally demonstrating that metropolitan dominance has not rendered rural electors irrelevant, just as a decade earlier they had thrown out Bjelke-Petersen, raises the question of the electoral check on political corruption. Clearly the end of the gerrymander has rendered this a practical consideration, unlike the situation in some states a generation ago, but other evidence suggests that it is a response as slow and ponderous as it is powerful, and it is hard to see how it could ever provide a speedy check. A move away from democracy as elected dictatorship seems highly unlikely.

It is easy to take a similar line with respect to political behaviour, especially at the state level. Less than twenty years ago what Fitzgerald was criticising was not a peculiarity of Queensland political behaviour, it was 'normal behaviour for many' (Bennett, 1992, 138). Parliamentarians and some bureaucrats were shocked by Fitzgerald – frightened may be a better word – in quite a different way from the general public. Abandonment of such political practices has often been reluctant, relapse not unknown, and their continuance can even be argued as integral to partisan political life. Conversely there is both evidence of improvement, scope for codes of conduct, and room for particular amelioration both formal and informal. Recall for example how weakly developed was the idea of conflict of interest and public interest during much of the two centuries of Australia's documented history, and the capacity of ICAC to at least draw attention to deficiencies in such areas as the parliamentarian's oath. Again the problem is largely that of maintaining a standard elevated, by considerable effort, after a particular incident or epoch.

Political behaviour is of course more than a matter of politicians and the public; it is also a matter of the public service in this context as more generally. An honest and effective bureaucracy is probably the most powerful of all anti-corruption measures. The Australian political tradition in this respect is mixed. The achievements must not be discounted, a functional democracy at almost every level and in almost every place and at almost every time over one hundred and fifty years. On the other hand there has been intermittent and widespread corruption and when the tradition of patronage has been superseded it has both been hard to prevent its re-emergence and to prevent the most wisely formulated alternative and innovations degenerating into systems dominated by seniority in staffing and sluggishness of process. A particular present concern is the run down, formal and informal, of the public service in the strict sense and its replacement by numerous consultants, contractors and advisers standing outside public service traditions and rules and in or close to the market place. This is a situation more likely to generate corruption than Australia's traditional public service ethos for all the latter's imperfections.

The conventional contemporary reaction to much of what I have written to this point is to emphasise accountability (and recall that this is an integral feature of the modern bureaucratic tradition) and openness and transparency (which is not, and is even less integral to the frequently advocated market alternative). As a Transparency International member and activist I am in no position to argue less than that these attributes of government, however hard to achieve, are of basic importance to corruption minimising governance. What constitutes accountability, openness and transparency is however much harder to define in any detail and implant in any organisation than to proclaim as a slogan. The most obvious risks belong to accountability, the construction of elaborate paper (or at least cyber) trails and over elaborate control mechanisms which focus attention away from the task in hand and onto at best corruption prevention and at worst onto avoiding detection. In either case an enormous slow down is the more likely outcome than achievement of either the sought after process or substantive objective. Transparency and openness too easily succumb to minimalist or illusionist interpretations. There is no obvious answer to these problems. I note however that the *Concise Oxford Dictionary* explains the word accountable in terms of responsibility and explicability, a crisper and more rational account than most of those who have hand on experience of any recent exercises in increasing or establishing accountability would provide. Might answerability be a better word? Letting the professional get on with the (well defined) job, treating him or her as such, moving away from his or her shoulder and getting off his or her back while relying on strict audit and the well protected whistleblower, would be my recipe for applied accountability.

Any discussion of the future must also recognise that it will be different, from which it follows that the structures designed to inhibit political corruption must be flexible and imaginative. Information technology provides the most obvious and immediately important example substantially if not completely capable of technical solution once its potential is adequately recognised. Secondly Australia remains and seems likely to remain an immigrant destination and a growing proportion of these immigrants is likely to come from countries where the status of political corruption is quite different from what it is or has been in either Australia or its traditional sources of immigration. How should Australia evaluate and respond to the probability that political corruption will be part of their baggage even when getting away from corruption is part of their motivation? A third issue follows from this. A more and more secular Australia still draws on the Judaeo-Christian tradition as a foundation of public and political morality. How durable is that situation in the context of a probable diminution of traditional religious belief and, equally important, knowledge and the entry of varieties of religious adherence of a presently minor character into the mainstream? Some of these faiths, Buddhism and Confucianism for example, have been viewed as part of the favourable context for the entrenchment of political corruption in Southeast Asia. It can be added in passing that an exploration of the ethnic and cultural background of participants in political corruption in contemporary Australia already a multicultural society would be of great interest. This is not to argue that the prospective dechristianisation of Australia must inevitably generate more political corruption but rather to indicate a context and connection – one among many – worth watching.

'Accountability and Corruption'

The preceding section presents an outsider's view, non-Australian, non-bureaucratic, the views of a non-politician with disciplinary affiliations and experience in an area not usually thought of as closely connected to either the themes of corruption in particular or of creating better and more effective government in general. How do they match up – or otherwise – with recent Australian thought in this area? For after all one of the issues intermittently raised, and in the latter part of the book asserted, as characteristic of contemporary Australia is the diminishing public acceptance of political corruption in Australia as normal and acceptable and an accelerating and growing emphasis on the need for radical change rather than piecemeal and *ad hoc* reaction and reform. The existence of substantive Australian works addressing this latter issue is not only a third major Australian contribution to the global scholarship of political corruption, to be placed alongside Hay and ICAC and like them combining empirical accounts and theoretical insight. It is also an opportunity to compare external evaluation grounded primarily in the domains of geography and history with the internal accounts – as well as prognoses and recommendations – of Australian scholars, administrators and politicians. For my own conclusions were drawn deliberately without detailed recent reference to the work in question, *Accountability and Corruption: Public Sector Ethics* (1997) (edited by Gordon Clark, himself a geographer specialising in public policy) and in its very title focused upon the broad themes of this book and a particular issue which may – or may not – provide the answer. There is of course an asymmetry in this approach: chapter 8 was written without particular recourse to Clark, but in writing this last section of that chapter on the basis of a rereading of Clark I am only too aware that that re-reading is with eyes and mind conditioned by the putting together of the preceding seven and a half chapters. I do not come to Clark cold. However I can state his book's, his diversity of contributors' positions, fairly and frankly, as well as noting areas of divergence and disagreement.

Clark's starting point is public reaction, aroused awareness and diminished tolerance, to the corruption crisis in Australia in the 1980s and 1990s, arguably a sometimes naïve reaction but also a general revulsion. This has in turn generated interest in public sector ethics and how its exploration may contribute to a raising of standards of political and administrative behaviour to more acceptable levels without I would add believing that this alone even in its most practical version will solve the problem. The discussion is evidently not reducible to matters of personal and individual honesty. Public service ethics, the most obvious path to political incorruptibility, is strewn with issues for administrators and representatives not so easily resolved, because the issues are public, are contested, and are in the last resort in some wise to be referred to the sovereignty of the people. The issues require both a coercive and educative approach.

Traditionally and even now Australians expect better of government than business in this respect but they are tending more and more to equate their expectations on the basis of the events and practices of the last two decades, many of them accurately called corrupt, both in means and ends. Government has also become less tolerant of minorities and dissent despite the obvious connection with core democratic values, and in much of its activity departs from traditional rules, norms and standards. Opportunistic executive power is now the norm with a considerable emphasis on control at the expense of toleration. To make matters worse bureaucrats share citizens' disillusion with politicians – as they long have – and may aspire to control the political agenda, at the politicians' expense, rather than service it. The result is a secretive approach to government, certainly not a transparent one, and obviously corruption prone. But father knows best, and may be prepared to get his hands dirty in the course of protecting what he sees as the public interest. A less than wholly naïve public calls much of this corruption, and a denial of true sovereignty or democracy. This position stated by Clark in chapter one is an essentially, I suspect exaggeratedly, dismal picture. What programmes do his fellow authors propose, and what do they regard as key issues?

If the first substantial topic addressed in the body of the book is the self-evidently and simply important matter of codes of conduct, general and specialised, yet the thrust of the discourse is at a more fundamental level. It should be noted however that at the 'down-to-earth' level almost half of the eighteen topics listed in the second chapter belong in the domain of political corruption. More interesting, more central to discussion of Australia's future, and more contentious both in theory and practice, are attempts to add or incorporate fundamental ethical principles, most notably those regarding respect for persons and the enforcement of such principles, into codes in particular and bureaucratic behaviour in general. Neither criminalisation of offence in this area, nor cost-benefit analysis offer a wholly satisfactory answer, and in my view the second is positively dangerous in this context. Whatever the process of enforcement tolerance as near to zero as possible is the best objective. The real problem is that Australians differ among themselves as to ethical principles and even liberal democratic theory, probably the most likely to be successful candidate for the role of generally acceptable political theory in Australia, is open to various and conflicting interpretations. This raises obvious problems in the area of recruitment and training of public servants and elected representatives even if we assume that individuals' ethical positions can and should be explored – and that they will tell the truth. 'Good government requires good people' (Clark *et al.*, 1997, 27), but what is good and where is it to be found? An endpoint of this argument, only too evidently, is a culturally monochrome bureaucracy run by a latter day inquisition. At the very least it may be necessary to exclude from public service and public office those of particular persuasions – but how? As earlier noted this problem will be accentuated by the dechristianisation and increasing cultural diversity of Australia. It should however be added that the problem of corruption clearly existed when Australia was overwhelmingly white and generally Christian at least in the loosest sense of the word. It cannot be blamed on cultural change but may still be harder to control or reduce in a rapidly changing cultural environment. Political corruption, its forms and extents, reflect the cultural environment, and perhaps Australia is getting as it got in the past, the political corruption it deserves, even while in private and public discourse a preference for something better is stated. That something better may require not codes of conduct or even ethical principles but fundamental cultural change, or even (dare it be said) cultural engineering. For a non-Australian to pursue that line any further would be grossly impertinent, beyond the comment that it can I believe be pursued without abandoning or destroying those Australian cultural virtues which so hugely outnumber Australian cultural vices. At the very least the matter needs discussion, especially with respect to inequalities, long recognised as a fundamental theme in discussion of political corruption. This debate must needs take place in a climate not only of divergent ethical and religious norms but in which the media stand accused of demeaning public standards – note however the central role of free media in exposing corruption – and where market forces appear more and more powerful and reluctantly challenged by mainstream political parties. The political class can scarcely be expected in these circumstances to take a role of ethical leadership. Who else will?

At a practical level (in Clark *et al.*, 1997, chapter 3) public service (as politics in general) is concerned with decision taking, generally, even at routine level, potentially corruptible (which is not to argue that this is the Australian norm) and for a substantial more senior minority involving unavoidable discretion, value judgement, and major decisions – even matters of life and death. At this point accountability enters the discussion. (It is of interest to note that this word along with others central to the discussion (e.g. interest groups, secrecy) appears often in the subject index. It is equally interesting that others similarly central but more diffuse in their treatment despite their centrality in the ethical context (e.g. trust) do not.) Accountability has been made more demanding by the alleged disarray of the traditional public service and the move towards administrative deregulation. (Or is the fundamental question, my view, that in practice accountability is reduced to a paper chase focused on backside protection, a distorted understanding of means triumphant over ends?) The key practical issues identified here have in the one case a long history – conflict of interest. The issue will never go away and is scarcely more difficult to manage in the future than the past. The second is 'whistleblowing', an issue central to corruption control, which might have but did not serve Australia well in the 1980s and which has proved extremely difficult to implement effectively in the face of political and public service resistance and a degree of public disdain. The sharp end of cultural values? Whether or not that is the case this may well be regarded as a key practical concern as far as the control of corruption is concerned as well as a useful indicator, in terms of degree of acceptance, of political health or malaise. At the very least a willingness to be accountable and practice accountability – in terms of responsibility, explicability and answerability – is a core ethical value which may reasonably be demanded of politicians, public servants and perhaps even citizens as political actors.

Subsequent chapters are of a more particular character without asserting fundamental dissent from the position that ethics matter. Hyde's quest for the identification of the proper degree of institutional autonomy rests on a view widely accepted by scholars of corruption that authoritarian states are inevitably corrupted. In terms of Australia's future this can be tuned into such questions as how much state authority (using state to cover all political levels) will optimise corruption levels at near zero, and what is the role of non-state institutions? Issues such as subsidiarity certainly have a place in any discussion of the future of corruption in Australia and the vision of Australia as a civil society rather than a client society might well be regarded as another generally acceptable core ethical value. In this context the role of NGOs as a bastion against corruption is of course again widely accepted though rarely articulated from the thoughtful libertarian position taken by Hyde.

One of the important contexts of corruption control in twenty-first century Australia (and more widely) is the focus of the seventh chapter: 'a diminution of confidence in the integrity of political leadership, public debate and the public policy process'. The discussion eventually, after a long discourse on the USA, reaches Fitzgerald's Queensland and WA Inc as issues of macro-mendacity complemented by the prevalence of political lying in general, discerned as a core feature of the loss of political confidence. Yet it is also one where there is evidence of bipartisan support, as seen in Queensland in 1995, for radical action. At first sight Mathew's proposal for an adjudicator-general 'who receives and investigates complaints of public falsehood and reports publicly to parliament' appears whimsical, much more so than proposals for the formal 'corruption proofing' of legislation and regulation (Perry, 1997, 124). On the other hand the costs and risks of 'experimentation are modest by comparison with the possible benefits of even partial success. The problem surely is that its introduction would be opposed and its operation obstructed by a still substantial number of politicians and, were it applied more widely, public servants. The proposal tends to assume or depend upon that higher level of political morality which it seeks to achieve. Mathew makes the interesting point however that certain kinds of parliamentary committees can and do operate in the non-partisan fashion required for this kind of operation. Moreover the obvious precedents, ombudsmen and ICAC, have met with considerable success despite strong opposition. 'Give it a go!'.

A less radical and more mainstream proposal is in the familiar territory of lobbying and its rapidly increasing role and significance. The right to make representation can be assumed, the ways and means are what are in question in the corruption context. Tongue (Clark *et al.*, 1997, chapter 8) records not only the increase and activity but the worst kind of half-hearted exercise in federal regulation – a voluntary and private register. (At least one is reassured by the knowledge that lobbyists are employed by CADs or PIGs (124).) Lobbying has its place but it is no substitute for open consultation and there is no guarantee of its truthfulness and it is open to accusations of favouritism (a form of corruption). What ethical demands can be made of lobbyists when and if they are seen as part of the political process, and how can they be enforced? Codes of conduct have a place here and some self-regulation is apparent, but so too is resistance. Yet another public office is one suggestion, in my view less attractive than the adjudicator-general. More fundamental change in the direction of effective registration and, with more difficulty, imposition of ethical standards is essential. One final comment; discussion here accepts, as I would, the legitimacy of lobbying but says nothing explicit about the need for limits. is There is here a whole area for debate. Who has the right, in what form (Caribbean cruises, cocktails, conferences?) and on what terms, is inadequately discussed and narrower in its focus than is required to explore or even sever the nexus between lobbying and corruption.

Secrecy is at the heart of corruption and the initial emphasis of the chapter on the topic (nine) upon political parties arguably exaggerates the extent to which the struggle for open government has been won. That focus is however upon a matter of immediate interest and ongoing significance. The evidence of corrupt practice in the affairs of Australian political parties across the spectrum is strong and if it continues is a threat to every other attempt to reduce corruption and to Australia's democracy in general. The situation arises from the fact that the parties compete for high stakes, that secrecy is a proven and powerful weapon in this competition, and that though an integral part of the political apparatus parties are in most respects private associations. So much is this so that it is at least debatable whether the goings on of political parties fall inside the stricter definitions of political corruption, even though common sense suggests that they should and the mainstream discussions of political corruption say at least something about party politics. Having stated a position Sherman proceeds however to talk mainly about secrecy in the executive branch, an excellent discussion but of what is on his own admission a secondary substance. That discussion does significantly relate to key corruption control issues, notably the whistleblower question where he notes 'hundreds of secrecy provisions that place significant barriers to public servant whistleblowers'. He also notes with approbation the bipartisan character of some key parliamentary committees, and with disapproval in the secrecy context, the growing private sector presence in government. Of most general interest is his caution as to the abundance of exceptions and provisos in measures designed to diminish secrecy and encourage openness. The point is of much wider significance for corruption control measures in general and likely to be the favoured self-defence weapon of vested interests. You have been warned! If openness be regarded as another ethical premise of good corruption 'free' government yet its implementation remains problematic.

The final substantive chapter (Clark *et al.*, 1997, chapter ten) asks how ethics should be promoted in a public service which experienced a crisis of self and public confidence in the 1980s, has been restructured in a fashion which calls into question older norms and standards which were a bulwark against corruption, and which must debate the particular roles of both formal conduct codes and the instilling into participants of ethical understanding. The question is more than simply dealing with or preventing abuse but of a positive role for government in the life of the nation. Russell is also profoundly aware of the historical context, Australian and global, an awareness not matched by all commentators and which must at least inform any action plan. More pessimistically but realistically Russell has problems in finding secure certain basic values receiving general acceptance in either the public service, especially its revamped and transformed version, or in society at large. The best on offer is to recognise that the two are connected. At least a preference for a public interest orientation as against nepotism and patronage can be practically assumed, and on such a basis five practical approaches are proposed: the limited but essential role of codes of conduct; effective and imaginative induction and training; positive socialisation (neither of these have been well handled in the past); role models and their celebration; and a culture of attention and action. The present problem results from a political leadership which in the eighties substituted arrogance for good judgement. Reform and renovation while requiring political support is a task for the public administrators themselves. Corruption control demands an input from public servants (and indeed the public) more than from party politics or consultants.

A lengthy conclusion (by a philosopher) argues a consequentialist – in essence cost-benefit – version of political ethics against the deontological rule based approach. Among other contributors only Corbett discusses (and rejects) this position. (Note again this important concept is unindexed.) This argument is unlikely to appeal to many scholars with a broad interest in political corruption. They will ask the questions 'whose cost and whose benefit', and demand exploration of alternatives. They may also question her view that 'consequentialism in public sector ethics gives *carte blanche* to all manner of ethical impropriety' is without serious foundation. What about Queensland in the 1980s, WA Inc, or the huge range of issues brought before ICAC – to say nothing of third world experience. Acceptance of her position does not doom Australia to an uncontrollable increase in political corruption but it seems to make it likely; at the very least it is a risky option in which an attractive path to challenge any exercise in corruption control is only too easily accessible, and true accountability compromised. If the book overall has a weakness it resides in a certain vagueness as to what really constitutes accountability. Where she may be agreed with is in her attack on the view that 'compliance with the letter of the law is all that need be done'. In St Paul's words 'the letter killeth but the spirit giveth life', and the law has the virtues but also the shortcomings of a schoolmaster.

There is a deal of common ground and consensus between the body of Australian experts concerned with a present 'crisis' and those of a New Zealander to whom the issue is one of intellectual concern and to be treated briefly, at times even hypothetically, at the end of an overview. Agreement exists in such diverse areas as the centrality of ethics, even with all the problems generated by recognising such a position, and so likewise of culture; the difficult task of the public servant in the present political climate; the significance of the regrettable reluctance of the public sector and political parties to be as cooperative as Clark and his contributors would have wished. Institutional reluctance to face hard questions remains well entrenched albeit in a defensive position. Our disagreement is on particulars and between individuals, notably on the potential and outcomes of cost-benefit analysis.

Whatever happens continuance of the *status quo*, seen as a strong bridgehead towards establishment of a significantly less corruption prone Australia, appears unlikely. Either the bridgehead will not merely be held but there will be a break out on the basis of popular support and in the direction of embedded institutional change, or the front will collapse into substantial retreat. The difficulty of such embedding and the implied cultural change is one reason for the existence of the second alternative, return to the situation which prevailed during the first three quarters of the twentieth century – and perhaps worse. This would be unfortunate but it would not be a catastrophe. It seems very unlikely that Australia will become an India let alone an Indonesia. Australians deserve better than any of these, but their wish to be well regarded as honestly governed has usually been accompanied by a corruption tolerance level too elevated for comfort and a resistance to corruption too slowly roused. It is too early to judge if the events of the 1980s and 1990s have durably changed this situation. Inevitably morality must be given the last word: as political corruption expresses the condition of public morality so the good health of the latter is the most fundamental bastion against the former. What this means is that Australia will get the corruption it deserves, and if morality – the distinction between right and wrong – is marginalised then corruption will move centre stage. I trust and hope this will not be Australia's experience.

Note

1   For a rare albeit non-Australian example see Perry (1997, 44-7). The fact that it had to appear as a fable, under threat of legal action, indicates one of the problems.

9 Updates

As already mentioned political corruption is almost constantly reported and discussed in the Australian media. The principal areas of attention at the time of final preparation of this book (early 2001) concern the affairs of the Australian Labour Party in Queensland as exposed before a Queensland Criminal Justice Commission enquiry (the Shepherdson Enquiry), and the universities.

Queensland

Allegedly the Queensland Labour party is and has been involved in a number of rorts and scams, driven by the notoriously factional structure of the party. These have primarily involved firstly the registration of voters at addresses where they did not in fact live or qualify in an attempt to win marginal seats. Members of parliament were actively involved but the newspaper reports do not suggest public service involvement. If allegations are true electoral law has been broken. Secondly the Labour Party has been accused of handing over money to rival smaller parties, Democrats and Greens, to obtain their preference votes – and thus enhance Labour's prospects – under Australia's preferential voting system. This is probably an offence under the Australian bribery laws, though prosecutions have been rare, the law is 'fuzzy', and proving intention – a key issue – is notoriously difficult. The broader context is of a Labour government with a tiny majority – now lost through the process of its own disciplining of members – and a real (but by Queensland standards modest) history of bribery allegations. Not yet and probably never a Fitzgerald!

One of these older allegations, concerning the allocation of gaming licences to supporters, belongs in the mainstream of political corruption strictly defined. The status of the present allegations under such definition is less clear since the breach of trust appears to have been by party rather than public officials. As noted earlier in the text the law traditionally regards political parties as private associations; their centrality to politics suggests that in fact they possess a public role bringing them within the definitional limit. In any case one of the allegations is being pursued under the bribery law.

What of course such a situation provides is a rich vein of comment, most of it along predictable lines. Although the party has disciplined offenders the remark 'but everybody does it' coupled with insider incomprehension indicates the power of the will to win, and the gulf between party professionals and enthusiasts and the man and woman in the street. The prediction that the affair will break the party is overstatement; similar previous events generated formal often bloody restructuring, a period of relative calm, and an eventual return to bad old ways. Editorial discussion, a little on the pompous side perhaps, nevertheless identifies such key issues as intent, secrecy, and betrayal of trust. The opposition of course uses the word corrupt, but it features much less than the standard Australian vocabulary of such occasions, rort and scam.

'Small earthquake in Brisbane – not many hurt' is a fair assessment. Maybe not much else was going on in late November/early December 2000. The goings on and the reportage do however illustrate important issues – the perennial even cyclical issue of corruption within parties and its status; the existence of central issues and a recognition of their centrality; and more optimistically a bipartisan media and public opinion with a now very modest tolerance of such shenanigans. 'The voters are entitled to know why parties that support transparency in politics find it acceptable to use loopholes in the electoral laws – 'because everyone else does it' – then find every reason they can to keep details out of the public domain.'

Universities

As the alleged electoral and party political rort in Queensland manifests an established and evidently ongoing dimension of political corruption in Australia, so the second breaking story of the first month of 2001 provides evidence and debate in a context which has hitherto featured rarely if at all in such discourse: education and more particularly university education.

Since the middle of January (2001) *The Sydney Morning Herald* has been running stories (and associated comment and correspondence, the latter nationwide) alleging malpractice, focused upon degree standards, which might be construed as political corruption. Within a week the affair had gained sufficient momentum to be reported internationally. The essence of the situation is allegations by academics that in some Australian universities, not for the most part the best known, academic standards and/or service provision are being compromised by passing full fee paying students who on academic performance should not have passed. Such students are in financial terms evidently more valuable than those in other categories who pay lower fees. The allegations are of instances where senior university management has overruled academic decisions – to pass or in these cases to fail – made by rank and file academic staff members. In the words of the headline to an article by a named academic (institution affiliation not given!): 'If at first you don't succeed make an offer'. (In fairness it should be added that though cases of simple bribery were mentioned in ensuing correspondence they were not a central issue.) As already noted the debate which followed indicated nationwide problems (even though it tended to concentrate on New South Wales and two of its universities) though not one present in every university.

Inevitably the existence of the problem was at best talked down and at worst denied when university managements entered the debate. The one important contextual point of agreement was the underfunding of the country's universities in the last two decades and the difficult relationship between tertiary sector and federal government. It would also be agreed, though not spelled out on this occasion, that whatever the status of Australia's tradition of political corruption it had rarely impinged upon the country's educational institutions. An occasional 'bad apple' would for once have been an accurate historical description. By comparison the connection and impact has been and remains conspicuous and significant in much of the third world as it was also in traditional communist régimes. Its peculiarly pernicious and damaging character has been commented upon (Perry 1997, 34, 39).

But is what has allegedly, and in my view probably, been going on in at least a few Australian universities political corruption? The essence of the case is that while universities are not in the strict sense parts of the state apparatus they are substantially (albeit inadequately) publicly funded on the basis of political decisions and also subject to a more general degree of political control. They are public institutions. By passing students who ought to fail in order to improve their own financial position the universities are in breach of their own objectives, as laid down in their foundation documents (commonly statutes) and working manuals, to say nothing of the less formal trust placed in them by their communities.

The question of breach of trust, one regarded as central to definitions of political corruption by most authorities, was raised in the media debate together with others which feature in academic discussion. (At the time of writing issues of equity and fairness had not.) Given that this was a debate not among such specialist authorities but on a wider canvas this (and similar issues discussed below) indicates an interesting and hopeful convergence of outlook between clerisy and laity of the subject. Among other such issues raised were those of the general condition of Australia's public morality, allegedly in decline; the status of the whistleblower and his/her protection, globally less satisfactory in universities than their essential purpose would suggest; and the changing university and student ethos in an age of marketisation and market forces, again driven more from outside than inside the universities.

The defensive reaction of the university authorities already noted firstly reveals that not all are prepared to undertake a full and frank discussion. Some are in denial, others in 'sweep it under the carpet' mode. At least initially, and at the time of writing, a wide ranging public enquiry has been refused (the Australian Universities Quality Agency is only in the process of formation) and the matter viewed as one for individual universities to enquire into. Another comment from a writer on university administration suggests, in my view unconvincingly, that this issue is nothing more than a misunderstanding of how the moderation of standards must work in cash strapped institutions. Generally the discussion from this quarter proceeds along the suspect 'bad apple' path.

In addition to the causes mentioned above others deserve to be taken seriously, preeminently the changed condition of universities and not least of their student body. Fee paying students and especially full fee paying students may in some cases (how many? how large a proportion?) see their position and payment as entitlement to a qualification rather than provision of an opportunity. The quest, largely international, for full fee paying students has brought into Australia's universities students from countries where attitudes to corruption are quite different from those of Australia and whose level of preparation for advanced study is poor. In these circumstances failure is likely and both parties are in search of a simple solution. If the allegations are true it would appear that the universities have been more active in this respect than the students. Finally to counter the risk of exaggeration, even reductionism, it must be pointed out that the question deserves to be set in the fullest and widest context: underfunding may be a very serious problem to managers, and to students it represents even in an environment where loans are readily available a pressing practical problem too often 'resolved' by a demanding 'part time' job to the detriment of study. This situation is an essential component of the matter of the failing student which is very much part of the issue under discussion.

Australia is one of several countries – New Zealand is another – where university education has become a major export industry, and that industry's success rests on reputation and is threatened by the present scandal. (The awful alternative is to accept and live with some educational Gresham's Law – bad coinage driving out good.) Australia cannot afford the complacency which has characterised the high level response to these allegations. Equally it would be perverse and ridiculous to assume extensive political corruption of academic standards, and the grapevine of university common rooms and conferences (which extends across the Tasman) would interpret the *Sydney Morning Herald* stories as indicative of serious local difficulties rather than general and endemic presence. I am unaware of such problems in my own university or more generally in New Zealand, but I certainly cannot be sure and hope both the system and I myself would react vigorously were such a problem to be alleged. The reporting and investigation of allegations, and the provision and exploration of structures and methodologies for their study is after all where corruption scholarship begins.

22 January 2001

Bibliography

Adams, F. (1893), *The Australians: A Social Sketch*, Fisher Unwin, London.

Alaba, R. (1994), *Inside Bureaucratic Power: the Wilenski Review of New South Wales Government*, Hale and Iremonger, Marrickville.

Alatas, S.H. (1990), *Corruption: Its Nature, Causes and Functions*, Gower, Aldershot.

Allingham, A. (1977), *Taming the Wilderness: The First Decades of Pastoral Settlement in the Kennedy District*, James Cook University of North Queensland (Studies in North Queensland History, no. 1), Townsville.

Andreski, S. (1966), *Parasitism and Subversion: The Case of Latin America*, Pantheon, New York.

Anon (probably Mugford, S.) (1981), 'Editorial: The Place of Corruption in Advanced Societies', *Australian and New Zealand Journal of Criminology*, vol. 14, pp. 193-6.

Atkinson, A. (1997), *The Europeans in Australia: A History*, Oxford University Press, Melbourne.

Atkinson, J. (1826), *An Account of the State of Agriculture and Grazing in New South Wales*, J. Cross, London. (1975 facsimile edition by Sydney University Press, Sydney.)

Atkinson, M. (1917), 'Notes on the Early Economic History of Australia', *JRAHS*, vol. 3, pp. 530-44.

'Australia: Terra Incognita' (1985), *Daedalus*, vol. 114 (1). (Special number of the *Proceedings of the American Academy of Arts and Sciences*.)

Australian Dictionary of Biography (1966-), Melbourne University Press, Melbourne. (In progress, complete to 1939.)

Baalman, J. (1962), 'Gubernatorial Land Jobbing', *JRAHS*, vol. 48, pp. 241-55.

Backhouse, J. (1843), *A Narrative of a Visit to the Australian Colonies*, Hamilton Adams, London.

Baker, D.W.A. (1958), 'The Origins of Robertson's Land Acts', *HS*, vol. 8, pp. 166-82.

Barnard, M. (1962), *A History of Australia*, Angus and Robertson, Sydney.

Barratt, A.H.B. (1979), *The Civic Frontier: The Origin of Local Communities and Local Government in Victoria*, Melbourne University Press, Melbourne.

Barrett, B. (1971), *The Inner Suburbs: The Evolution of an Industrial Area*, Melbourne University Press, Carlton.

Bate, W. (1978), *Lucky City: The First Generation at Ballarat 1854-1901*, Melbourne University Press, Carlton.

Bate, W. (1983 – second edition), *A History of Brighton*, Melbourne University Press, Melbourne.

Bennett, S. (1992), *Affairs of State: Politics in the Australian States and Territories*, Allen and Unwin, Sydney.

Bernays, C.A. (1919), *Queensland Politics During Sixty (1859-1919) Years*, Government Printer, Brisbane.

'Bigge Report' (1822), *Colony of New South Wales: Report of Commission of Enquiry* (British Parliamentary Papers, 1822, xx).

Blainey, G. (1969 – second edition), *The Rush That Never Ended: A History of Australian Mining*, Melbourne University Press, Melbourne.

Boehm, E. (1971), *Prosperity and Depression in Australia 1887-1897*, Clarendon, Oxford.

Bok, S. (1978), *Lying: Moral Choice in Public and Private life*, Harvester, Hassocks.

Bok, S. (1984), *Secrets: Concealment and Revelation*, Oxford University Press, Oxford.

Bolton, G.C. (ed.) (1986-88), *Oxford History of Australia*, Oxford University Press, Melbourne (4 vols).

Boot, H.M. (1998), 'Government and the Colonial Economies', *AEcHR*, vol. 38, pp. 74-101.

Boot, H.M. (2000), Reply to Frost, L. (2000), *AEcHR*, vol. 40, pp. 86-91.

Booth, E.C. (1869), *Another England: Life, Living, Homes and Home Makers in Victoria*, Virtue, London.

Borrow, K.T. (1984), 'Bentham, Colonel Torrens, "Self Supporting Colonisation" and the South Australian Real Property Act', *SA*, vol. 23, pp. 54-125.

Bottom, B. (1987), *Connections II: Crime Rackets and Networks of Influence in Australia*, Sun Books, South Melbourne.

Bowes, K.R. (1968), *Land Settlement in South Australia*, Libraries Board of South Australia, Adelaide.

Buggy, H. (1977), *The Real John Wren*, Widescope, Camberwell.

Burnley, I.H. (ed.) (1974), *Urbanization in Australia: The Post-war Experience*, Cambridge University Press, London.

Burroughs, P. (1967), *Britain and Australia 1831-1855: A Study in Imperial Relations and Crown Lands Administration*, Clarendon,

Oxford.

Butlin, N.G. (1994), *Forming a Colonial Economy, Australia 1810-50*, Cambridge University Press, Cambridge.

Buxton, G.L. (1967), *The Riverina 1861-1891: An Australian Regional Study*, Melbourne University Press, Carlton.

Cannon, M.P. (1967), *The Land Boomers*, Melbourne University Press, Melbourne.

Carboni, Rafaello (1855 – 1963 edition), *The Eureka Stockade*, Melbourne University Press, Carlton.

Carroll, J. (1957), 'The Sceptic Turns Consumer: An Outline of Australian Culture', *Quadrant*, vol. 22, pp. 11-5.

Charlton, P. (1983), *State of Mind: Why Queensland is so Different*, Methuen Haynes, North Ryde.

Clark, G.L., Jonson, E.P., Caldow, W. (eds) (1997), *Accountability and Corruption: Public Sector Ethics*, Allen and Unwin, St Leonards.

Clarke, F.G. (1989), *Australia: A Concise Political and Social History*, Harcourt, Sydney, 1989.

Clarke, Marcus (1870 – Penguin 1979), *His Natural Life*, Penguin, Harmondsworth.

Coaldrake, P. (1989), *Working the System: Government in Queensland*, Queensland University Press, St Lucia.

Coaldrake, P. and Wanna, J. (1989), '"Not Like the Good Old Days": The Political Impact of the Fitzgerald Enquiry into Police Corruption in Queensland', *Australian Quarterly*, vol. 60, pp. 404-14.

Coghlan, T.A. (1918), *Labour and Industry in Australia*, Oxford University Press, London (4 vols).

Collis, E.H. (1948), *Lost Years: A Backward Glance at Australian Life and Manners*, Angus and Robertson, Sydney.

Commonwealth of Australia (1984), *Royal Commission on the Activities of the Federated Ship Painters and Dockers Union* (being the 6th and final report), 5 vols and appendices, Canberra. (The Costigan Report.)

Cornish, P. (1998), *An Overview of the History, Role and Function of the Anti Corruption Branch*, South Australian Police, unpublished.

Costigan Report, see Commonwealth of Australia (1984).

Coward, D. (1969), 'Free Selecting on the Emmerella Shore', *JRAHS*, vol. 55, pp. 355-79.

Crowley, F.K. (1971), *Forrest 1847-1918, Vol. 1, 1847-91. Apprenticeship to Premiership*, Queensland University Press, St Lucia.

Daly, M.T. (1982), *Sydney Boom, Sydney Bust: the city and its property market 1850-1981*, Allen and Unwin, Sydney.

Davidson, G. (1970), 'The Expansion of Melbourne in the 1880s', *AEcHR*, vol. 10, pp. 169-89.

Davis, S.R. (ed.) (1960), *The Government of the Australian States*, Longmans, London.

della Porta, D. and Vannucci, A. (1999), *Corrupt Exchanges: Actors, Resources and Mechanisms of Political Corruption*, Aldine de Gruyter, New York.

Denholm, B. (1980), *The Irrepressible Mr Dooley*, published by the author, Howrah.

Dickie, P. (1988), *The Road to Fitzgerald*, Queensland University Press, St Lucia.

Dilke, Sir Charles (1868 first edition, 1890 second edition), *Problems of Greater Britain*, Macmillan, London (2 vols).

Dunstan, D. (1984), *Governing the Metropolis: Melbourne 1850-1891*, Melbourne University Press, Carlton.

The Economist (1843-), London.

Eddy, J.J. (1969), *Britain and the Australian Colonies 1818-1831: The Technique of Government*, Clarendon, Oxford.

Encel, S. (1970), *Equality and Authority: A Study of Class, Status and Power in Australia*, Cheshire, Melbourne.

Epps, W. (1894), *Land Systems of Australasia*, Swan Sonnenschein, London.

Evans, W.P. (1969), *Port of Many Prows*, Hawthorn, Melbourne.

Finn, P. (1987), *Law and Government in Colonial Australia*, Oxford University Press, Melbourne.

Finnane, M. (1994), *Police and Government: Histories of Policing in Australia*, Oxford University Press, Melbourne.

Fitzgerald, R. (1982), *A History of Queensland from the Dreaming to 1915*, Queensland University Press, St Lucia.

Fitzgerald, R. (1984), *A History of Queensland from 1915 to the 1980s*, Queensland University Press, St Lucia.

Fitzgerald Report, see Queensland (1989).

Fitzgerald, S. (1987), *Rising Damp: Sydney 1870-90*, Oxford University Press, Melbourne.

Fitzgerald, S. (1992), *Sydney 1842-1992*, Hale and Iremonger, Sydney.

Fletcher, B. (1979 (1)), 'Administrative Reform in New South Wales under Governor Darling', *AJPA*, vol. 38, pp. 246-62.

Fletcher, B. (1979 (2)), '"Born Bureaucrat": Thomas Cudbert Harrington', *AJPA*, vol. 38, pp. 263-78.

Forrest, M. (1979), 'Public Administration and the Executive', in Perran, R. and Shearman, C. (eds), *Essays in West Australian Politics*, University of West Australia Press, Nedlands, pp. 64-96.

Forsyth, W.D. (1970 – second edition), *Governor Arthur's Convict System: Van Diemen's Land 1824-36: A Study in Colonization*, Sydney

University Press, Sydney.

Friedrich, C.J. (1974), *The Pathology of Politics: Violence, Betrayal, Secrecy, Corruption and Propaganda*, Harper and Row, New York.

Frost, L.E. (1986), 'A Reinterpretation of Victoria's Railway Construction Boom of the 1880s', *AEcHR*, vol. 26, pp. 40-55.

Frost, L.E. (2000), 'Government and the Colonial Economies: An Alternative View', *AEcHR*, vol. 40, pp. 71-85. (See also Boot, H. (2000).)

Gammage, B. (1990), 'Who Gained and who was Meant to Gain from Land Selection in New South Wales', *HS*, vol. 24, pp. 104-22.

Gibbons, P.C. (1940), 'The administration of Governor Hunter', *JRAHS*, vol. 26, pp. 403-17.

Gill, J.H.C. (1971), 'Thomas Peel: The Dream that Became a Nightmare', *Journal of the Royal Historical Society of Queensland*, pp. 154-72.

Grabosky, P.N. (1977), *Sydney in Ferment: Crime, Dissent and Official Reaction 1788 to 1973*, ANU Press, Canberra.

Gray, I. (1991), *Politics in Place: Social Power Relations in an Australian Country Town*, Cambridge University Press, Cambridge.

Hagger, J. and Montanelli, T. (1980), *Consolidated Index to the Checklist of Royal Commissions, Select Committees and Boards of Inquiry held in the Commonwealth of Australia, Queensland, New South Wales, South Australia, Tasmania and Victoria 1856-1960*, La Trobe University Library Publication no. 19, Bundoora.

Hallows, J. (1970), *The Dreamtime Society*, Collins, Sydney.

Hancock, W.A. (1930), *Australia*, Benn, London.

Hardy, F.J. (1951, third unexpurgated edition), *Power Without Glory*, Realist Printing and Publishing, Melbourne.

Hardy, F.J. (1963), *Legends from Benson's Valley*, Werners Laurie, London.

Hardy, F.J. (1971), *The Outcasts of Foolgarah*, Melbourne, Allara.

Harling, P. (1996), *The Waning of 'Old Corruption': The Politics of Economical Reform in Britain 1779-1846*, Clarendon, Oxford.

Hasluck, Sir Paul (1977), *Mucking About: An Autobiography*, Melbourne University Press, Carlton.

Hawker, G. (1979), 'An Investigation of the Civil Service: the South Australian Royal Commission of 1888-91', *JRAHS*, vol. 65, pp. 46-58.

Hay, P.R. (1977), 'Factors Conducive to Political Corruption: The Tasmanian Experience', *PS*, vol. 29, pp. 115-30.

Head, B. (ed.) (1986), *The Politics of Development in Australia*, Allen and Unwin, Sydney.

Heidenheimer, A.J., *et al.* (1989), *Political Corruption: A Handbook*, Transaction, New Brunswick.

Heller, A. and Feher, F. (1988), *The Post-Modern Political Condition*, Columbia University Press, New York.

Hirst, J.B. (1973), *Adelaide and the Country 1870-1917: Their Social and Political Relationship*, Melbourne University Press, Carlton.

Hirst, J.B. (1983), *Convict Society and its Enemies*, Allen and Unwin, Sydney.

Hogue, J.A. (1907-9), 'Governor Darling, the Press, and the Collar', *JRAHS*, vol. 2, pp. 308-22.

Hollander, R. (1997), '"Contracting": the Queensland Housing Commission Experience 1945-57', *AEcHR*, vol. 37, pp. 118-36.

Hughes, O.E. (1999 – third edition), *Australian Politics*, Macmillan, South Yarra.

Hughes, R. (1987), *The Fatal Shore: A History of the Transportation of Convicts to Australia, 1787-1868*, Collins, London.

ICAC (1989-), Annual Report, Sydney.

ICAC (1990), *Report on Investigation into North Coast Land Development*, Sydney.

ICAC (1991 (1)), *Report on Investigation Concerning Neal and Mochalski*, Sydney.

ICAC (1991 (2)), *Report on Investigation into the Planning and Building Department of South Sydney Council*, Sydney.

ICAC (1991 (3)), *Report on Investigation into Sutherland Licensing Police*, Sydney.

ICAC (1991 (4)), *Report on Investigation Relating to Stait Dainford and Waverley Council*, Sydney.

ICAC (1991 (5)), *The First Two Years: Nineteen Key Issues*, Sydney.

ICAC (1992 (1)), *Corruption Prevention Project: Allocation of Boat Moorings by the New South Wales Waterways Authority*, Sydney.

ICAC (1992 (2)), *Report on Investigation into Local Government, Public Duties and Conflicting Interests*, Sydney.

ICAC (1994), *Investigation into the Relationship between Police and Criminals: Second Report*, Sydney.

ICAC (1995), *Report on Investigation into Randwick City Council*, Sydney.

ICAC (1995-), *Corruption Matters*, Sydney.

ICAC (1997 (1)), *Community Attitudes to Corruption and the ICAC 1996*, Sydney.

ICAC (1997 (2)), *Encouraging New South Wales Public Sector Employees to Report Corruption*, Sydney.

ICAC (1997 (3)), *Monitoring the Impact of the New South Wales Protected Disclosures Act 1994*, Sydney.

ICAC (1997 (4)), *Report on Investigation Concerning the 1993 Byron Residential Strategy and Associated Matters*, Sydney.

ICAC (1997 (5)), *Report on the Conduct of George Bertoucello ...*, Sydney.

ICAC (1998 (1)), *A Major Investigation into Corruption in the Former State Oil Authority of New South Wales*, Sydney.

ICAC (1998 (2)), *Report on Investigation into Aboriginal Land Councils in New South Wales: Corruption Prevention and Research Summary*, Sydney.

ICAC (1998 (3)), *Report on the Investigation into the Conduct of an Alderman on Fairfield City Council*, Sydney.

ICAC (1999), *Report on Investigation into Aboriginal Land Councils in New South Wales: Investigation Report*, Sydney.

ICAC (2000) *Rebirthing Motor Vehicles: Investigation into the Conduct of Staff of the Roads and Traffic Authority and Others*, Sydney.

Jackson, M. and Smith, R. (1996), 'Inside Moves and Outside Views: An Australian Case Study of Élite and Public Perceptions of Political Corruption', *Governance*, vol. 9, pp. 23-42.

Jackson, R.V. (1998), 'The Colonial Economies: An Introduction', *AECHR*, vol. 38, pp. 1-15.

Jaensch, D. (ed.) (1986), *The Flinders History of South Australia: Political History*, Wakefield, Netley.

Jaensch, D. and Teichmann, M. (eds) (1994 – fourth edition), *The Macmillan Dictionary of Australian Politics*, Macmillan, South Melbourne.

Jeans, D.N. (ed.) (1986-87), *Australia: a Geography* (2 vols), Sydney University Press, Sydney. (Volume 1 (1986), *The Natural Environment*; Volume 2 (1987), *Space and Society*.)

Johnson, L., Logan, W.S. and Long, C. (1998), 'Jeff Kennett's Melbourne: Post Modern City, Planning and Politics', Sydney. (Paper given at the International Planning History Conference, 1998.)

Johnston, R.J. (1980), *The Geography of Federal Spending in the United States of America*, Research Studies Press, Chichester.

Kennedy, K.H. (1978), *The Mungana Affair*, Queensland University Press, St Lucia.

Kennedy, K.H. (1979), 'Bribery and Political Crisis, Queensland 1922', *AJPH*, vol. 25, pp. 66-76.

Kiddle, M.L. (1961), *Men of Yesterday: A Social History of the Western Districts of Victoria*, Melbourne University Press, Melbourne.

King, C.J. (1957), 'An Outline of Closer Settlement in New South Wales: Part 1, The Sequence of the Land Laws 1788-1956', *Review of Marketing and Agricultural Economics*, vol. 25, 290 pp.

Knight, K. (1961), 'Patronage and the 1894 Royal Commission of Inquiry into the New South Wales Public Service', *AJPA*, vol. 7, pp. 166-85.

Knight, K. (1972), 'Patronage and the New South Wales Public Service: The 1894 Royal Commission', in Crook, D.P. (ed.) *Questioning the Past: A Selection of Papers in History and Government*, Queensland University Press, St Lucia.

Kriak-Krai, J. (1971), *Corrupt Practices in the State and Local Governments of New South Wales*, University of Sydney, M.Ec. thesis 1971. (Access restricted.)

Lack, C. (ed.) (1962), *Three Decades of Queensland Political History 1929-1960*, Government Printer, Brisbane.

Lang, J.T. (1956), *I Remember*, Invincible, Sydney.

Larcombe, F.A. (1973, 1976, 1978), *A History of Local Government in New South Wales*, Sydney University Press, Sydney (3 vols).

Laverty, J.R. (1972), 'Metropolitan and Central Government in Queensland 1859-1925', in Crook, D.P. (ed.) (1972), *Questioning the Past: A Collection of Papers in History and Government*, Queensland University Press, St Lucia, pp. 262-81.

Lloyd, E. ('A Squatter') (1846), *A Visit to the Antipodes with Some Reminiscences of a Sojourn in Australia*, Smith Elder, London.

Loveday, P. and Martin, A.W. (1966), *Parliaments Factions and Parties: The First Thirty Years of Responsible Government in New South Wales*, Melbourne University Press, Carlton.

Lovell, D.W., McAllister, I., Maley, W. and Kukathas, C. (1995), *The Australian Political System*, Longman, Melbourne.

McAdam, A. and O'Brien, P. (1987), *Burke's Shambles: Parliamentary Contempt in the Wild West*, Burke Press, Melbourne.

McCalman, J. (1984), *Struggletown: Public and Private Life in Richmond 1900-1965*, Melbourne University Press, Carlton.

McCulloch, S.C. (1959), 'Unguarded Comments on the Administration of New South Wales 1839-1846, the Gipps-La Trobe private correspondence', *HS*, vol. 9, pp. 30-45.

MacIntyre, S. (1985), *Winners and Losers: The Pursuit of Social Justice in Australian History*, Allen and Unwin, Sydney.

McKay, A. (ed.) (1962), *Journals of the Land Commissioners for Van Diemen's Land 1826-28*, University of Tasmania and Tasmania Historical Research Association, Hobart.

MacKenzie, J. (1962), *Australian Paradox*, MacGibbon and Kee, London.

McLachlan, M.D. (1969), 'Bathurst at the Colonial Office 1812-27: A Reconnaissance', *HS*, vol. 13, pp. 477-502.

McMartin, A. (1983), *Public Servants and Patronage: The Foundation and Rise of the New South Wales Public Service*, Sydney University Press, Sydney.

McMartin, A. (1987), 'Patronage, Merit and Mortality', in Eddy, J.J. and

Nethercote, J.R. (eds) (1987), *From Colony to Coloniser: Studies in Australian Administrative History*, Royal Australian Institute of Public Administration, Sydney.

McQuilton, J. (1979), *The Kelly Outbreak 1878-1880: The Geographical Dimension of Social Banditry*, Melbourne University Press, Carlton.

Maiden, A.N. (1991), 'Construction's Big Hole in Your Pocket', *Independent Monthly*, Surry Hills, New South Wales, vol. 2, pp. 261-2.

Maiden, H.E. (1966), *The History of Local Government in New South Wales*, Angus and Robertson, Sydney.

Mayer, H. and Nelson, H. (eds) (1973), *Australian Politics: A Third Reader*, Cheshire, Melbourne.

Mayer, H. and Nelson, H. (eds) (1980), *Australian Politics 5*, Longman, Melbourne.

Mayne, A.J.C. (1982), *Fever Squalor and Vice: Sanitation and Social Policy in Victorian Sydney*, Queensland University Press, St Lucia.

Meinig, D.W. (1962), *On the Margins of the Good Earth: The South Australian Wheat Frontier 1869-1884*, Rand McNally, Chicago.

Meudell, G. (1929), *The Pleasant Career of a Spendthrift*, Routledge, London.

Moir, P. and Eijkman, H. (eds) (1992), *Policing Australia; Old Issues – New Perspectives*, Macmillan, South Melbourne.

Morgan, S. (1992), *Land Settlement in Early Tasmania: Creating an Antipodean England*, Cambridge University Press, Cambridge.

Morison, J. ('A Clergyman') (1968 – second edition), *Australia in 1866*, Longmans, London.

Morison, J. ('A Clergyman') (1894 – third edition), *Australia as it is, or Facts and Features, Sketches and Incidents of Australia and Australian Life with Notices of New Zealand*, Longmans, London.

Morrison, W.F. (1888), *The Aldine Centennial History of New South Wales*, Aldine, Sydney (2 vols).

Mudie, J. (1837), *The Felonry of New South Wales etc. (1837)*, Angus and Robertson, London.

Murphy, D.J. (1977-8), 'The Premiers of Queensland', *Queensland Historical Journal*, vol. 10, pp. 87-109.

Murphy, D.J. and Joyce, R.B. (eds) (1978), *Queensland Political Portraits 1859-1952*, Queensland University Press, St Lucia.

Myrdal, G. (1968), *Asian Drama: An Enquiry into the Poverty of Nations*, Penguin, London.

Nairn, B. (1967), 'The Political Mastery of Sir Henry Parkes: New South Wales Politics 1871-1891', *JRAHS*, vol. 53, pp. 11-51.

New South Wales (1883), *Report of the Inquiry into the State of the Public Lands and the Operation of the Land Laws*, Sydney.

New South Wales (1892), *Report of the Royal Commission into Charges Against Mr E.M.G. Eddy, Chief Commissioner of Railways*, Sydney.

New South Wales (1906 (1)), *Report of the Royal Commission into the Administration of the Lands Department*, Sydney.

New South Wales (1906 (2)), *Report of the Royal Commission of Inquiry into the Administration of Crown Lands*, Sydney.

New South Wales (1911), *Legislative Council: Report of the Royal Commission on the Department of Public Works*, Sydney.

New South Wales (1931), *Report of the Royal Commission on the Administration of the Western Division of New South Wales*, Sydney.

Noonan, J.T. (1984), *Bribes*, Macmillan, New York.

O'Brien, P. (ed.) (1986), *The Burke Ambush: Corporatism and Society in Western Australia*, Apollo, Nedlands.

O'Brien, P. (1988), 'West Australia Inc.: A State of Corruption', *Quadrant*, vol. 32, no. 250, pp. 4-18.

O'Brien, P. (1990), 'The Last Laugh: Western Australia's Elections and the Executive State 1983-89', *Politics*, vol. 25, pp. 113-30.

O'Hara, J. (1988), *A Mug's Game: A History of Gaming and Betting in Australia*, New South Wales University Press, Kensington.

Parker, R.S. (1978), *The Government of New South Wales*, Queensland University Press, St Lucia.

Parkes, Sir H. (1892), *Fifty Years in the Making of Australian History*, Longman, London.

Parsons, T.G. (1974), 'Public Money and Private Enterprise: The Administration of the New South Wales Commissariat, 1813 to 1820, *JRAHS*, vol. 60, pp. 1-11.

Patience, A. (ed.) (1985), *The Bjelke-Petersen Premiership 1968-1983: Issues in Public Policy*, Longman, Melbourne.

Peachment, A. (ed.) (1991), *The Business of Government: Western Australia 1983-1990*, Federation Press, Annandale.

Pearl, C.A. (1958), *Wild Men of Sydney*, W.H. Allen, London.

Perry, P.J. (1997), *Political Corruption and Political Geography*, Ashgate, Aldershot.

Perry, P.J. (1994), 'Corruption and Geography: A Fable', *Applied Geography*, pp. 291-3.

Phillips, M. (1909), *A Colonial Autocracy: New South Wales under Governor MacQuarie*, King, London.

Philp, M. (1997), 'Defining Political Corruption', *PS*, vol. 45, pp. 436-62.

Pike, D. (1957), *Paradise of Dissent: South Australia 1829-1857*, Longmans, London.

Pilger, J. (1989 first edition, 1992 second edition), *A Secret Country*, Cape London-Vintage, London.

Powell, J.M. (ed.) (1973), *Yeomen and Bureaucrats: The Victorian Crown Lands Commission 1878-79*, Oxford University Press, Melbourne.

Prasser, S., Wear, R. and Nethercote, J. (1990), *Corruption and Reform: The Fitzgerald Vision*, Queensland University Press, St Lucia.

Price, A. Grenfell (1924), *The Foundation and Settlement of South Australia 1829-1845*, F.W. Preece, Adelaide.

Pringle, J.D. (1958), *Australian Accent*, Chatto and Windus, London.

Quaife, G.R. (1969), 'Make Us Roads No Matter How: A Note on Colonial Politics', *AJPH*, vol. 15, pp. 47-54.

Queensland (1900), *Report of the Royal Commission to Inquire into the Administration of the Department of Public Works etc.*, Brisbane.

Queensland (1956), *Report of the Royal Commission into Allegations of Corruption Relating to Dealings with Certain Crown Leaseholds*, Brisbane.

Queensland (1989), *Report of a Commission of Enquiry Pursuant to Orders in Council*, Brisbane. (The Fitzgerald Report.)

Queensland CJC (1991), *Report on a Public Enquiry made into Payments made by Land Developers to Aldermen and Candidates for Election to the Council of the City of Gold Coast*, Brisbane.

Queensland CJC (1994), *Report on an Investigation into Complaints Against Six Aboriginal and Island Councils*, Brisbane.

Radbone, I. (1981), 'Interview with a Former Public Service Commissioner Mr L.C. Hunkin', *SA*, vol. 20, pp. 65-98.

Rafaello, Carboni. (See Carboni.)

Ranken, G. (1893), *Our Wasted Heritage*, publisher and place of publication unknown.

Reinits, R. and T. (1967), 'The Broughton Case', *THRAPP*, vol. 15, pp. 33-44.

Reynolds, H. (1969), '"That Hated Stain": The Aftermath of Transportation in Tasmania', *HS*, vol. 14, pp. 19-31.

Richards, E. (ed.) (1986), *The Flinders History of South Australia: Social History*, Wakefield, Adelaide.

Ritchie, J. (1970), *Punishment and Profit: The Reports of Commissioner John Bigge on the Colonies of New South Wales and Van Diemens Land 1822-23; Their Origins, Nature and Significance*, Heinemann, Melbourne.

Roberts, S.H. (1924), *History of Australian Land Settlement 1788-1920*, Melbourne University Press, Melbourne.

Roberts, S.H. (1934, republished 1964), *The Squatting Age in Australia*, Melbourne University Press, Carlton.

Robinson, M.E. (1976) *The New South Wales Wheat Frontier 1851-1911*, ANU (publication HG/10), Canberra.

Robinson, P. (1985), *The Hatch and Brood of Time: A Study of the First Generation of Native-Born White Australians* (vol. 1), Oxford University Press, Melbourne.

Robson, L. (1983 and 1991), *A History of Tasmania*, Oxford University Press, Melbourne (2 vols.).

Rose, L.N. (1922), 'The Administration of Governor Darling', *JRAHS*, vol. 8, pp. 97-176.

Rose-Ackerman, S. (1999), *Corruption and Government: Causes, Consequences and Reform*, Cambridge University Press, Cambridge.

Sachier, M. and Storrier, S.A. (1965), 'As Others Saw Us', *JRAHS*, vol. 51, pp. 213-48.

Sandercock, L. (1975), *Cities for Sale*, Melbourne University Press, Carlton.

Sandercock, L. (1979), *The Land Racket: The Real Costs of Property Speculation*, Hale and Iremonger (for Australian Association of Socialist Studies), Sydney.

Semmler, C.W. (1984 – second edition), *The Banjo of the Bush: The Life and Times of A.B. Paterson*, Queensland University Press, St Lucia.

Serle, G. (1963), *The Golden Age: A History of the Colony of Victoria 1851-1861*, Melbourne University Press, Parkeville.

Serle, G. (1971), *The Rush to be Rich: A History of the Colony of Victoria 1883-1889*, Melbourne University Press, Melbourne.

Shaw, A.G.L. (1967), 'Some Officials in Early Van Diemen's Land', *THRAPP*, vol. 14, pp. 129-41.

Shaw, G.P. (1976), 'The Political Career of William Broughton', *AJPA*, vol. 22, pp. 338-46.

Shelden, M. (1991), *Orwell: The Authorised Biography*, Heinemann, London.

Sheldon, P. (1993), 'Public vs. Private Employers on New South Wales Public Works 1890-1910', *AECHR*, vol. 33, pp. 49-72.

South Australia (1865), *Report of Select Committee of the House of Assembly ... Selling the Crown Lands*, Adelaide.

South Australia (1890), *Report on Disposal of Crown Lands in South Australia*, Adelaide.

South Australia (1927 (1)), *Report of the Second Royal Commission on Allegations of Bribery against Police Officers*, Adelaide.

South Australia (1927 (2)), *Police Bribery Royal Commission – Report of Commissioner of Police on findings*, Adelaide.

Stannage, C.T. (1979), *The People of Perth: A Social History of Western Australia's Capital City*, Carroll's for Perth City Council, Perth.

Stannage, C.T. (ed.) (1981), *A New History of Western Australia*, University of West Australia Press, Nedlands.

Statham, P. (1984), 'The Role of the Commissariat in Early West Australian Economic Development', *AEcHR*, vol. 24, pp. 20-33.

Statham, P. (1990), 'A New Look at the New South Wales Corps', *AEcHR*, vol. 30, pp. 43-63.

Stein, R. (1981), 'Sir Robert Torrens and the Introduction of the Torrens System', *JRAHS*, vol. 67, pp. 102-18.

Steketee, M. and Cockburn, M. (1986), *Wran: An Unauthorised Biography*, Allen and Unwin, Sydney.

Swanton, B. (1985), 'Commissioner James Mitchell: A Biographical Sketch', *JRAHS*, vol. 70, pp. 280-7.

Tasmania (1910 (1)), *Lands Department Commission*, Hobart.

Tasmania (1910 (2)), *Report of the Royal Commission on the Scottsdale-Branxholm Railway*, Hobart.

Taylor, G.P. (1967), 'Business and Politics in Queensland 1859-95', *New Zealand Journal of History*, vol. 1, pp. 75-92.

Terrill, R. (1987), *The Australians: In Search of an Identity*, Bantam, London.

Therry, R. (1863), *Reminiscences of Thirty Years Residence in New South Wales and Victoria*, Sampson Low, London.

Tiffen, R. (1999), *Scandals, Media, Politics and Corruption in Contemporary Australia*, University of New South Wales Press, Sydney.

Townsley, W.A. (1991), *Tasmania: from Colony to Statehood*, St David's Park, Hobart.

Townsley, W.A. (1994), *Tasmania: Microcosm of the Federation or Vassal State 1945-1983*, St David's Park, Hobart.

Trollope, A. (1873), *Australia and New Zealand*, Chapman and Hall, London. (Page references are to 1967 Queensland University Press edition.)

Troy, P.N. (1978), *A Fair Price: The Land Commission Program 1972-77*, Hale and Iremonger, Sydney.

Turner, H.G. (1904), *A History of Victoria ...*, Longmans, London (2 vols).

Twopenny, R. (1883 – Penguin 1973), *Town Life in Australia*, Elliot Stock, London.

Victoria (1930), *Royal Commission on the City of Williamstown.* (Unpublished – typescript available in Victorian parliament.)

Victoria (1933), *Report of Board of Inquiry ... Police Force*, Melbourne.

Victoria (1978 (1)), *Board of Enquiry into Certain Land Purchases by the Housing Commission*, Melbourne.

Victoria (1978 (2)), *Report of Board of Inquiry into Allegations Against Members of the Victoria Police Force*, Melbourne.

Walker, R.B. (1958), 'Squatter and Selector in New England 1862-95', *HS*, vol. 8, pp. 66-79.

Waller, P. (1974), 'Groups, Parliaments and Selections: Tasmanian Politics in the 1890s', *THRAPP*, vol. 21, pp. 89-103.

Ward, J.M. (1963), 'Historiography' in McLeod, A.L. (1963), *The Pattern of Australian Culture*, Oxford University Press, Melbourne.

Ward, R.W. (1978), 'The Australian Legend Revisited', *Historical Studies*, vol. 18, pp. 171-90.

Ward, R.W. (1987), *Finding Australia: The History of Australia to 1821*, Heinemann, Richmond.

Waterson, D.B. (1968), *Squatter, Selector and Storekeeper: A History of the Darling Downs 1859-1893*, Sydney University Press, Sydney.

Waterson, D.B. (1984), *Personality, Profit and Politics: Thomas McIlwraith in Queensland 1866-1894*, Queensland University Press (John Murtagh Macrossan Lecture 1978), St Lucia.

Weller, P. (ed.) (1994), *Royal Commissions and the Making of Public Policy*, Macmillan, South Melbourne.

West Australia (1901), *Reports of the Royal Commission on the Railway and Customs Department of West Australia*, Perth.

West Australia (1902 (1)), *Report of the Royal Commission Appointed to Inquire into and Report upon the Conduct and Completion of the Coolgardie Water Scheme*, Perth.

West Australia (1902 (2)), *Report of the Select Committee of the Legislative Council on the Metropolitan Water Works*, Perth.

West, J.T. (1852), *The History of Tasmania* (edited and with introduction by Shaw, A.G.L. 1981), Angus and Robertson, Sydney.

Whip, R. and Hughes, C.A. (eds) (1991), *Political Crossroads: the 1989 Queensland Election*, Queensland University Press, St Lucia.

Whitelock, D. (1977), *Adelaide 1836-1976: A History of Difference*, Queensland University Press, St Lucia.

Wild, R.A. (1974), *Bradstow: A Study of Status, Class and Power in a Small Australian Town*, Angus and Robertson, Sydney.

Williams, R. (1999), 'Democracy, Development and Anti-Corruption Strategies: Learning from the Australian Experience', *Commonwealth and Comparative Politics*, vol. 37, pp. 135-48.

Wright, R. (1989), *The Bureaucrat's Domain: Space and the Public Interest in Victoria 1836-84*, Oxford University Press, Melbourne.

Wurth, W.C. (1960), 'The Public Service, Board of New South Wales since 1895', *JRAHS*, vol. 45, pp. 289-313.

Zalums, E. and Stafford, H. (1980), *A Bibliography of West Australian Royal Commission, Select Committees of Parliament, and Boards of Enquiry 1870-1979*, published by the authors, Blackwood.

Index

For Product Safety Concerns and Information please contact our EU
representative GPSR@taylorandfrancis.com Taylor & Francis Verlag GmbH,
Kaufingerstraße 24, 80331 München, Germany

Printed and bound by CPI Group (UK) Ltd, Croydon, CR0 4YY
08/06/2025
01896999-0001